'Round the world cooking library

Central European Cooking

Original recipes from Switzerland, Austria, Czechoslovakia, Hungary and Rumania

Recipe contributions
by Eva Bakos
author of 'Wiener Spezialitäten'
and Albert Kofranek
author of 'Die gute Wiener Küche'

GALAHAD BOOKS • NEW YORK

Contents

3 At the Table in Central Europe
12 Entrees
16 Cheese dishes
19 Soups
26 Dumplings
28 Fish dishes
40 Meat dishes
61 Poultry and game dishes
68 Vegetable dishes
76 Desserts
92 Beverages
94 Kitchen terms
94 Alphabetical index
97 Index by type of dish

Cup measures in this book are based on an eight ounce cup.

Recipe contributions: Eva Bakos, author of 'Wiener Spezialitäten' and Albert Kofranek, author of 'Die gute Wiener Küche's and Ferenc Dergacz, Monimpex, Budapest, Hungary
American editor: Irena Kirshman, graduate Cordon Bleu Cooking School, lecturer on international cuisines, food consultant
Associate American editor: Susan Wright

Editorial staff for 'Round the world cooking library
Project editor: Wina Born, Dame de la Chaîne des Rôtisseurs and member of the board of the Fédération Gastronomique
Executive editor: Ton van Es
Text editor U.S.A.: Martin Self B.A., J.D.
Cover photo: Henk van der Heijden, Amsterdam
Photos p. 4: Swiss Travel Agency
Photos pp. 5, 12 (below), 32 (top), 36 (below), 40, 41, 44 (below), 45, 48, 49, 53, 65 (below), 77: Kremayr & Scheriau, Vienna, Austria
Photos pp. 8, 9: Han Born, Amsterdam
Photos pp. 16, 25 (top), 85: Ed Suister, Amsterdam
Photos p. 28: Monimpex, Budapest, Hungary
Photos pp. 25 (below), 29 33, 36 (top), 37, 52, 56, 57, 61, 64, 68, 69, 72, 73, 76: Conny van Kasteel, Milan, Italy
Design and drawings: Rosemarijn van Limburg Stirum, Amsterdam
Created by: Meijer Pers B.V., Amsterdam, The Netherlands
Typeset by: Service Type Inc., Lancaster, Pennsylvania and Internationaal Zetcentrum B.V., Wormerveer, The Netherlands
Printed by: Drukkerij Meijer B.V., Wormerveer, The Netherlands
Bound by: Proost en Brandt N.V., Amsterdam, The Netherlands
Publisher: Drake Publishers Inc., New York, N.Y.
Distributor: Galahad Books, New York, N.Y.

At the table in Central Europe

The vast region called Central Europe stretches from the snow-covered peaks of the Alps, along the wide valley of the Danube through Austria and the wide plains of Hungary, to the dark woods of the Carpathian Mountains in Rumania. The area is a patchwork of countries, of peoples and languages, of religions and cultures. It includes Switzerland, Austria, Czechoslovakia, Hungary and Rumania; its' people speak French, German and Italian as well as Czech, Slovak, Hungarian and Rumanian; and they are Lutherans, Calvinists, Roman Catholics and Greek Orthodox. The culinary traditions of this vast region are as varied as the landscape itself. Each nation has its own special dishes, though over centuries contact between the countries has been close.

Switzerland

Switzerland, a small country with towering mountains and crystal-clear lakes, has long been known as the 'playground of Europe.' In summer, mountain climbing, hiking, boating and swimming delight visitors; in winter, skiing and other winter sports in the Alps attract vacationers from all over the world. Because of international tourism, Switzerland has naturally become a country known for its hotels and its great hotel tradition. Young people come from all over Europe to learn the hotel business in special Swiss hotel schools or by working in the hotels themselves. In fashionable winter sport resorts such as St. Moritz and Pontresina, famous luxury hotels serve their guests sophisticated international cuisine (in fact, French). But the old Swiss dishes are not entirely lost, and guests at small hotels and village inns can still enjoy the traditional cooking of Switzerland.

Before tourism (and banking) made Switzerland a rich country, it was very poor, so poor, in fact, it could hardly feed its own people. Men from the villages traditionally fought outside Switzerland as mercenaries. Swiss Guards once served the Kings of France, and today they still protect the Pope in the Vatican Palace. Little can grow in the Alps that cover so much of Switzerland, and Swiss cooking has had to be sober and

In October, grapes for the blond Swiss wines ripen on the sunny southern slopes overlooking Lake Geneva.

Emmenthal cheeses are as big around as wagon wheels. They are often the pride and joy of the 'Senn', cattle herders who make these cheeses in their Alpine huts high in the mountains.

simple. But at the same time it is rich in calories, to compensate for working in the freezing winter and climbing the heights. Formerly, many villages and remote farms in the Alps were inaccessible for months because of heavy snowfalls. This isolation forced the Swiss to make the best out of what they could produce at home and keep through the winter: potatoes grown on the rocky soil, cheese from dairy herds and dried fruit from small local orchards.

It is hard, though, to speak of a single national cuisine in Switzerland. Because it is a small country, bordered on all sides by larger ones, Switzerland is strongly influenced by all the nations around it. This is true even in speech. There are three principal languages spoken in Switzerland: German in the north and center, French in the west and Italian in the south. And it is also true in cooking. The dishes of northern and central Switzerland resemble those of neighboring South Germany very closely. Here there are cosy taverns where foamy beer in large mugs accompanies hard, spicy garlic sausages that make one thirst for even more beer. The 'Dürre Landsjäger' ('dry gendarme'), 'Knackerlis' (small spicy sausages), or 'Bindenfleisch' (made of meat dried in the cold mountain air and thinly sliced) are only a few examples. The two best known dishes of

German-speaking Switzerland are 'Berner Platte', prepared with different kinds of sausages and pork with sauerkraut; and 'Züricher Ratsherrentopf' ('dish of the councillors of Zürich'), also prepared with a wide variety of meats. From western Switzerland come many recipes based on cheese, which is no wonder, since this is the land of the renowned Gruyêre and Emmenthaler cheeses. The famous Swiss fondue, made from cheese melted in white wine, no doubt originated in this region. Here, farmers in their mountain huts also make substantial cheese soups by putting a layer of grated cheese in a bowl, breaking an egg over it and then pouring in a boiling broth containing slices of potatoes and onions. In southern Switzerland, which extends like a sunny Alpine balcony above Italy, the cooking is strongly Italian, with spaghetti and macaroni, polenta, minestrone and stuffed pig's foot. But anywhere you go in Switzerland, there are delectable fish such as the 'omble chevalier' (a variety of perch), which comes from Lake Geneva, and the 'felchen' (a member of the salmon family)

from the Lake of Zürich; both are prepared in a delicious thick sauce of fresh cream. And everywhere, too, are cakes and pies, mostly made with fruit or with the famous Swiss chocolate.

Austria

Austrian cooking means Viennese cooking. Vienna has always been a city of restaurants, cafes, coffee houses and, above all, 'Konditoreien', pastry shops where you can eat cakes and drink coffee. And the imperial splendor of Vienna still lives on.

Although the last Emperor abdicated in 1918, two enormous palaces remain: the ancient and stately Hofburg in the center of the city, and the graceful, rococo Schönbrunn in its delightful park on the city's outskirts. Vienna continues to be a place with style and elegance, a city which has conserved some of the carefree atmosphere that reigned in its imperial past.

The Viennese begin their day and crisp bread. They eat little first thing in the morning because later, at about 10:30, the Viennese have a 'Gabelfrühstuck' (fork breakfast), preferably in a cozy café. This can consist of a plate of goulash or a bowl of cold meat with a horseradish sauce, or often warm sausages with mustard or kidneys in cream sauce. With a good glass of beer, this will hold them over until lunch at about one o'clock. Lunch begins with soup, most likely a broth with an enormous 'Knödel' (a dough ball) floating in the middle. The favorite main dish is stewed meat in a sour cream sauce prepared with onions and paprika (the Hungarian influence on Austrian and especially Viennese cooking is strong), and potatoes or noodles. But the Viennese appetite is still not satiated. A sweet dessert follows, which the Austrians call 'Mehlspeise' (literally flour dish), a matter-of-fact name for the enticing variety of cakes in which the Viennese housewife excels.

These include 'Schmarn', a kind of pancake prepared with a lot of eggs, 'Knödel', in which many apricots and plums find their place, 'Palatschinken', thin pancakes and 'Strudel'. At four o'clock it is time for coffee again, taken in one of the large, old-fashioned coffee houses that have been the home to generations of poets, composers and philosophers. Here the specialty is 'Wiener Melange', a

The Austrian winemaking school is established in Klosterneuburg, an ancient town north of Vienna. The town is surrounded by a veritable 'sea' of vineyards. Top quality Austrian wines are still left to age in wooden barrels; according to tradition, these are often carved with artistic and playful designs.

Czechoslovakia

large glass of coffee with a glob of whipped cream on top. Coffee can also be drunk in one of the 'Konditoreien', followed by such delicious Viennese cakes as 'Krapfen' or 'Kipferl', or perhaps the 'Linzertorte' (which comes from Linz and not from Vienna) or the rich brown 'Sachertorte.' The evening meal is understandably modest, often only cold meat with bread. But as far as eating is concerned, the day is far from over. At the opera there is a fashionable buffet where you can drink champagne and eat caviar, smoked trout or smoked goose breast sandwiches, as well as simpler buffets with warm sausages, potato salad and beer. And to end the evening in a really festive way we can go on to Sacher's Hotel. For supper there is crispy, fried 'Wiener Backhendl' (a very young deep-fried chicken) or cold trout with a bottle of cool white Austrian wine.

Czechoslovakia is a country known for its beer and sausages. The art of sausage-making is nowhere brought to a higher peak of perfection. These sausages taste best eaten in one of the many 'beer gardens' all over Czechoslovakia, where the whole family spends beautiful summer days and evenings. In origin, Czechoslovakian cooking is a mixture of German and Slavic traditions. The Germans contributed the 'knedliky' (a Slavic form of the German word 'Knödel'). These come in all shapes and sizes, from small balls to large egg-shaped rolls. They can be found in soup or accompanying meat, and can also have a sweet plum or other fruit filling. Czechs are also fond of smoked meat, usually served with a heavy sauce made with sour cream and grated horseradish. Wild mushrooms are a particular favorite, gathered in Bohemia's extensive forests. At the end of the summer and during the fall, mountain mushrooms appear in all the markets, and almost every kitchen has a long rope of dried mushrooms hanging from the ceiling. Not only mushrooms come from these woods, but also game: Czechoslovakia is a paradise for hunters, and there are no better hares, deer, pheasants and grouse anywhere in Europe. But the most festive dishes that do honor to Czechoslovakian cooking are carp in black sauce and, above all, goose. No village is complete without geese. At Christmas time, they can weigh more than 25 pounds and make up the main course of the family meal.

Hungary

Along with the French and the Italians, the Hungarians have one of the great cuisines of Europe. The Hungarians themselves are descendants of the fierce horsemen who migrated from the distant steppes of Central Asia in the 9the century and settled on the vast plains of Hungary because they were reminded of the flat expanses of their homeland. Hungarians to this day speak a language which has very little resemblance to any other European tongue, and which is also incredibly difficult to learn. The people have a unique national character; they are energetic, very intelligent, musical, and possessed with a melancholy only forgotten in the presence of good food, good drink and good gypsy music. The importance which Hungarians place on good food and drink is matched in Europe only by the French. And just as has happened in France, appreciation of food and inventiveness in cooking have created a great restaurant tradition. It is almost impossible to eat badly in Hungary. No matter where you dine, whether in the elegant restaurants of Budapest, the small outdoor cafes on Lake Balaton or the remote farms of the Hungarian plain, the food is lovingly prepared, and a gypsy violinist is almost always present to supply the flowing melodies that accompany the food.

Paprika is often said to be at the heart of Hungarian cooking. But it is in fact not indigenous to Hungary. It was the Spaniards who brought paprika back from the New World in the 16th century, the Portuguese who traded paprika seeds in Venice, the Greeks who then sold them to the Turks, and the Turks, then ruling over Hungary and the Balkans, who planted the seeds in their gardens. But this was still the hot pepper, called the 'Turkish pepper' in Europe, that came from Mexico. In the 19th century, Hungarians experimented with the plant and obtained a noble paprika of a clear red color, a piquant flavor and aroma, but which was not at all hot. They called it the sweet paprika. These grow in southern Hungary and reach their bright red ripeness in September. They are picked and brought in to the small farms where they are put on strings and hung on the chalk-white walls to dry. When they are finally crisp and dry, the paprikas are ground to a powder. During the three weeks the paprikas are drying, the farming villates are festively decorated with glowing red wreathes of paprikas hung everywhere in the warm autumn sun. Walking through a paprika village is like walking through a sunset, with the penetrating deep red peppers hanging down the walls and garden fences. In addition to these sweet paprikas there is still another variety, the cherry paprika. The fruit is round instead of oblong in shape, but it is incredibly hot. These small cherry paprikas find their rightful place in a famous carp soup that tastes best in the fishermen's villages along the Danube. The soup is cooked in large pots hanging on a tripod over an open fire, and it has the fiery red color that comes from the paprika. Horsemen on the vast plains cook their goulash in the same way, and in the evenings the setting sun takes on the same glowing red as the paprika-flavored goulash in the pots.

Hungary is a fertile land of abundant harvests, with hot, dry summers and long sunny autumns. Hungary's wheat makes some of the best bread in all of Europe, and corn and sunflower seeds are fed to pigs and poultry, making these unequaled in flavor and tenderness. The warm sun also provides sweet juicy fruit and golden wines. The richness of the land is reflected in the traditional Hungarian farmer's breakfast: a small glass of apricot brandy to wake up with, good peasant bread with paprika rolled up in strips of bacon and a raw yellow paprika and slices of delicious hard, piquant salami.

Rumania

Rumania is bordered on the west by Hungary, and Transylvania, the area between the Hungarian border and the Carpathian Mountains, was for centuries a part of Hungary. It is not surprising then that Rumanian cooking has a Hungarian flavor, with red paprika everywhere. But Rumania also has its own culinary tradition, and one important element in it is 'mamaliga', or as the Rumanians affectionately call it, 'mamaligutsa.' This is a thick porridge made of coarse cornmeal, something like Italian polenta. But since Rumanians have their own special kind of corn and their own individual way of cooking it, 'mamaliga' is unique. Rumanian country women bring 'mamaliga' to the table on a wooden board. From the board hangs a string used to cut through the thick porridge.

In Rumania 'mamaliga' is served with just about everything, much as potatoes find their place in almost every meal in the rest of Europe. But the classic combination remains 'mamaliga' with fresh white sheep's cheese, poached eggs and thick sour cream.

To get to know Rumanian cooking at its best, it's necessary to be invited to a Rumanian peasant wedding. October is the prime wedding month.The hogs, geese, turkeys and chicken have been fattened through the summer, the young wines have

A picturesque village street in Czechoslovakia. The Hungarian winemaster has tapped wine out of the barrel to be tasted with an implement called the 'loppe' (which literally means the thief).

In October, the red paprikas are plucked in Hungary; they are then hung in long chains on the walls of the houses to dry. When they are thoroughly dry, they are ground into powder and can be bought in the shops as spicy 'edelsüsz' paprika.

just been put in the cellars, the corn has been harvested and the October weather is still beautiful. At a real Rumanian wedding there are at least a hundred guests, and they can thus be served only at hotels or around long tables with wooden benches outside the farmhouse. The wedding celebrations last for three days and three nights: from Friday evening until Monday afternoon.

Behind the house, meat is cooked, fried and roasted, large pots of soup simmer and geese, chicken and turkeys turn on the grill. The large vats of wine and plum brandy stand on the porch and are constantly being used to refill the pitchers on the tables. At every wedding there are gypsy musicians: two violinists, a bass player, a zither player and almost always a female singer. These musicians lead the betrothed to the church before the wedding and after the ceremony lead the newly-weds away to the celebrations.

The Rumanians acquired their love of eating outside from their contact with the Turks. Each Rumanian city has at least one outdoor restaurant, and in the capital, Bucharest, there are

A Rumanian country wedding is a three-day long feast. There are usually at least a hundred guests and the food is cooked in large pots in the open air. While the gypsies sing and dance, everyone finds a place around the long tables and eats his fill of traditional wedding dishes washed down with wine and plum brandy.

dozens. Guests sit under the trees. There is always a large charcoal grill smoking away, and the other aromas that reach one, the smell of roasting meat and plum brandy, are equally appetizing. On beautiful summer evenings, Rumanians sit for hours in these outdoor restaurants where they drink and talk and eat and hum along with the music of the gypsy orchestra. The Rumanians have an untranslatable word for this pleasurable state – 'kef' – which means an atmosphere of good feeling, of being together with friends, of enjoying oneself eating and drinking. It is this 'kef' that kindles an inevitable nostalgia in all Rumanians who go abroad; a nostalgia also felt for 'mamaligutsa', for the aroma of 'mititei' (small rolls of garlic-seasoned ground meat, roasted over a charcoal fire) and for the taste of plum brandy.

Wines and liqueurs

Vineyards grow in all the countries of Central Europe. In Switzerland they dot the low, Alpine foothills and the lakesides, especially lakes Geneva and Neuchâtel. The wines are excellent, for the grapes are nourished not only by the sun directly, but also by its reflection in the clear waters. Although Switzerland has a few good red wines such as the fruity Dôle from the valley of the Rhône, most Swiss wines are white. There are dry crisp wines from Neuchâtel, and sparkling wines which hold their own against real champagne. And there are also delectable white wines from along Lake Geneva, and, of course, the best known of all, Fendant, from the canton of Valais. The Swiss also make a very good liqueur from the cherries that grow around the peak called the Rigi. This is an indispensable ingredient in 'fondue.'

Austria is also a country for great white wines. They grow not only in the beautiful, romantic valley of the Danube, but also on the hillsides outside Vienna and along the shores of the Neusiedlersee in the southeast. These white Austrian

wines are full-bodied and flavorful, and they have the fruity taste of ripe grapes. The Austrians, and especially the Viennese, often drink very young wines, not yet a year old, called 'Heurige.' They go to the cosy wine cellars and gardens of villages along the Danube and in the woods outside Vienna. Winemakers who gladly receive guests for the 'Heurige' hang out bunches of evergreens or straw wreathes from their houses. From Vienna the visitor can take the streetcar to the small wine villages in the nearby hills: to Grinzing, Nussdorf or to Heiligenstadt. It's a good idea to take a picnic lunch along, and it's possible, in fact, to buy special 'Heurige' baskets in many Vienna delicatessens. On beautiful evenings people sit on long wooden benches at wooden tables under the trees in the gardens. There is always a 'Schrammel' orchestra with a violinist, zither and harmonica players and a vocalist who sings all the old-fashioned, sentimental Viennese songs.

Hungary is a country of fabled wines renowned since the Middle Ages. One such wine is Egri Bikavér, 'bull's blood', from the city of Eger: a fiery, strong deep-red wine whose history dates back to at least the 16th century. Another is the famed Tokay, from a town of the same name in eastern Hungary. Golden, sweet Tokay is a wine with legendary powers: the imperial family of Austria had a special vineyard and wine cellars in Tokay where their personal wines grew and were stored. These Tokays were always given to expectant mothers in the imperial family to give them stamina. Tokay is still used in Hungarian hospitals, where it is given to patients suffering from physical exhaustion and weakness. Hungary also has other great white wines which grow along the shores of the Lake Balaton. The vines take advantage of a double sun: the sun in the sky and the almost equally bright one reflected in the lake. In another region of Hungary, a delicious brandy is made from juicy apricots. It is so strong that after 24 hours the empty glasses have acquired a delicious apricot perfume. This apricot brandy, called 'barack palinka', was a favorite drink of the Duke of Windsor.

Czechoslovakia is a beer country. In the city of Pilsen the breweries have become so famous that the name 'Pils' or 'Pilsener' has entered many languages as a word meaning light lager beer. The Rumanians are wine drinkers par excellence, gifted with wine in abundance; for small Rumania is Europe's fifth-ranking wine producer. Every kind of wine comes from the country's vineyards: from cool, light white wines to full, heavy red wines and golden honey-sweet dessert wines. The Rumanians also make a famous plum brandy called 'tsuica'. This is a very refined brandy always drunk as an aperitif. In the winter, when the Carpathian Mountains are covered with snow and the wolves come down to the valleys, the people sit around a coal fire eating 'sarmalutse', small cabbage rolls filled with ground meat, while they drink 'tsuica fiarte', glowing hot plum brandy with black pepper. Anyone not warmed up by this drink must have a heart of ice.

Piquant egg dishes, either hot or cold, are always favorites in Austria. Eggs Tyrolean style.

Filled eggs (recipe page 14, 1st column)

Tiroler Eierspeise

Eggs Tyrolean style

4 servings

- *4 large potatoes, cooked, peeled and sliced*
- *4 hard boiled eggs, sliced*
- *4 anchovies, drained and chopped*
- *2 tablespoons finely chopped parsley*
- *½ cup heavy cream*
- *¼ teaspoon salt*
- *Freshly ground black pepper*
- *½ cup dried breadcrumbs*

Butter an ovenproof casserole and arrange ⅓ of the potato slices on the bottom. Cover with a layer of ½ the eggs and anchovies. Repeat the layers and top with the remaining potato slices. Sprinkle with 1 tablespoon parsley. Combine the cream, remaining parsley, salt and pepper and pour over the potatoes. Sprinkle the breadcrumbs on top and bake in a 350° oven for 30 minutes. Serve from the casserole.

Solothurner Käseschnitte

Cheese sandwiches from Solothurn

4 servings

- 8 *slices day-old white bread, crusts removed*
- ¼ *cup dry white wine*
- 4 *tablespoons softened butter*
- 8 *thick slices soft cheese*
- 1 *teaspoon paprika*
- 1 *teaspoon cumin*

Brush the slices of bread on one side with wine. Spread the other side with butter. Arrange the slices, buttered side up, on a baking sheet. Place 1 slice of cheese on each piece of bread and sprikle with paprika and cumin. Bake in a 350° oven for about 10 minutes until cheese is melted.

Cheese sandwiches from Solothurn Switzerland's limited agriculture is mainly suited to dairy farming, which means, of course, that Swiss cooking is full of cheese dishes.

Gefüllte kalte Eier

Filled eggs

4 servings

Aspic:

1 (15 ounce) can chicken broth
1 egg white, lightly beaten
Shell of 1 egg
1 package unflavored gelatin
2 tablespoons water

8 hard boiled eggs
2 gherkins, finely chopped
½ cup finely chopped ham
2 teaspoons chopped capers
½ teaspoon tomato paste
½ teaspoon prepared mustard
1½ tablespoons mayonnaise
Few drops Worcestershire sauce
¼ teaspoon salt
Freshly ground black pepper
2 tablespoons chopped chives

To prepare the aspic, combine the broth, egg white and egg shell in a saucepan. Beating vigorously with a wire whisk, bring the mixture to a boil. Stop beating, lower the heat and simmer 10 minutes. Carefully strain the broth through several layers of cheesecloth into a bowl. Sprinkle the gelatin over the water to soften. Add the gelatin to the warm broth, stirring to dissolve. Chill the aspic while preparing the eggs. Cut the eggs in half. Remove the yolks and place in a bowl with all the remaining ingredients except the chives. Combine thoroughly and stuff the egg whites with the mixture. Sandwich the egg halves together and arrange on a serving dish. When the aspic is syrupy, spoon a thin layer over the eggs and chill them. When the first layer is set, spoon more aspic over the eggs. Repeat several times more. Sprinkle the chives over the eggs and serve.

Gerollte Eierspeise

Rolled eggs

4 servings

¾ cup breadcrumbs
½ cup milk
2 cups minced chicken or veal
1 cup minced ham
¾ teaspoon salt
Freshly ground black pepper
2 egg yolks, beaten
4 eggs, beaten
2 tablespoons butter

Soak the breadcrumbs in milk. Stir in the chicken, ham, salt, pepper and egg yolks. Form into a sausage-like roll 2 inches in diameter. Butter a large piece of aluminum foil. Wrap the roll in foil and steam over boiling water for 1½ hours until firm. Beat the eggs with a little salt. Heat 2 tablespoons of butter in a large skillet, pour in the eggs and prepare a flat omelette. Remove from the pan. Roll the omelette around the steamed chicken, cut into 1 inch slices and secure each slice with a toothpick. Serve hot.

Böhmer Eierspeise

Bohemian eggs

6 servings

6 eggs
2½ cups water
1½ tablespoons salt
Coarsely ground black pepper
½ cup shredded onion skins
2 teaspoons caraway seeds

Boil the eggs gently for about 8 minutes. Rinse under cold running water. Gently tap the shells so they are evenly cracked on all sides. Place the eggs in a pan with the 2½ cups water, salt, pepper, onion skins and caraway seeds. Bring to a simmer and cook 5 minutes. Remove from the heat and let the eggs stand in the seasoned water at least 8 hours. Drain, peel and cut in half lengthwise. Serve on individual plates.

Kartoffelsalat

Potato salad

4 servings

1 pound small new potatoes
½ teaspoon salt
Freshly ground black pepper
2 tablespoons olive oil
1½ tablespoons vinegar
1 tablespoon grated onion
1 tablespoon finely chopped parsley
1 teaspoon chervil
½ tablespoon chopped chives
2 gherkins, finely chopped

Cook the potatoes with their skins on in boiling, salted water 20 to 30 minutes or until tender. Drain and peel while still hot. Slice the potatoes and place in a bowl. Add all the remaining ingredients except the gherkins and toss gently. Refrigerate 2 to 3 hours. Sprinkle the chopped gherkins over the salad before serving. This is excellent served with smoked trout or salt herring.

Rindfleischsalat

Meat salad

4 servings

2 cups diced cooked meat
2 cooked potatoes, diced
2 tomatoes, peeled, seeded and chopped
1 small onion, chopped
2 gherkins, chopped
½ teaspoon mild (Dijon type) mustard
1 tablespoon vinegar
3 tablespoons oil
¼ teaspoon salt
Freshly ground black pepper
¼ cup mayonnaise
2 hard boiled eggs, sliced
1 tablespoon chopped chives

Combine the meat, potatoes, tomatoes, onion and gherkins in a salad bowl. With a wire whisk, beat the mustard, vinegar, oil, salt and pepper together and toss the salad with the dressing. Garnish with the mayonnaise and eggs and sprinkle the chives on top.

Körözött

Cottage cheese spread

4 servings

½ pound cottage cheese
⅓ pound butter, softened
¼ teaspoon salt
Freshly ground black pepper
1 teaspoon sweet paprika
½ teaspoon mild (Dijon type) mustard
1 tablespoon grated onion
1 teaspoon caraway seeds, crushed
2 anchovies, finely chopped
2 teaspoons chopped capers

In a bowl, beat the cottage chesse and butter until creamy. Add salt, pepper, paprika, mustard, onion, caraway seeds and anchovies. Beat until very smooth and creamy. Chill 2 hours before serving.

Cheese dishes

According to tradition, cheese fondue was created by a Swiss winegrower's wife during the vintage. As she was very busy picking grapes, she had no time to prepare the normal type of meal.

Cheese fondue is now probably as popular abroad as it is in Switzerland itself. But its origins are uniquely Swiss. Fondue was most likely invented by a wine grower's wife somewhere near Neuchâtel during the weeks of the grape harvest. This has always been a very busy time for the whole family, and the work is hard. There is no time to prepare a full meal, but everyone must still eat heartily to cope with the grape picking. The famer's wife hit upon the idea of melting cheese in wine in a large pan and setting it in the middle of the table. Everyone would sit around the pan, dipping pieces of bread stuck onto a fork into the soft, hot cheese mixture and enjoying a substantial meal prepared quickly. Because cheese fondue is so easy to make, and with no dishes to wash afterwards, it has naturally become popular around the world in recent years. But it needs a healthy stomach to digest this heavy mixture. Therefore, it's important to remember to add Kirsch (cherry liqueur) to make the fondue easier to digest. And it's also a good idea to drink hot tea with the fondue; this helps it go down more easily.

Fondue

Cheese fondue

6 servings

- *1 clove garlic, cut in half*
- *2 cups dry white wine*
- *1 pound Gruyère cheese, grated*
- *1 pound Emmenthal (Swiss) cheese, grated*
- *Freshly ground black pepper*
- *3 tablespoons cornstarch dissolved in 3 tablespoons kirsch*
- *1 loaf French bread, cut into cubes*

Rub garlic all over the inside of an earthenware fondue pot. Pour in the wine and place over moderate heat until the wine begins to bubble. Add the cheese a little at a time, stirring constantly as if making a figure 8. When the cheese has melted, sprinkle with pepper and stir in the dissolved cornstarch. Place the fondue pot over a portable burner at the table. Provide each guest with a long fork. (A bread cube is speared on the fork and dipped into the melted cheese.) Serve a dry white wine with the fondue.

Käse Beignet

Cheese steak

8 servings

- *1¾ cups flour*
- *1 cup beer*
- *⅔ cup water*
- *2 egg whites*
- *8 ½ inch thick slices Gruyère cheese, each weighing about 2 ounces*
- *½ cup flour for dredging*
- *Oil for deep frying*

Sift the flour into a bowl. Add the beer and water and beat until smooth. Cover and let the batter stand 1 hour. Beat the egg whites until soft peaks form and fold into the batter. Dredge each cheese slice in flour and dip into the batter. Fry the cheese in hot (375°) oil until golden brown. Drain on paper towels and serve immediately.

Gâteau au fromage Fribourgeoise

Cheese pie from Fribourg

4 to 6 servings

- *1½ cups flour*
- *½ teaspoon salt*
- *6 tablespoons butter*
- *4 tablespoons water*
- *2 tablespoons butter*
- *1 onion, chopped*
- *2 cups grated Gruyère cheese*
- *4 eggs, beaten*
- *½ teaspoon salt*
- *Freshly ground black pepper*
- *⅛ teaspoon nutmeg*
- *1 cup light cream*

Place the flour and salt in a bowl. Blend in the butter with a pastry blender until it resembles fine breadcrumbs. Add the water and stir with a fork to form a smooth dough. Roll out the pastry ⅛ inch thick and line a 9 inch pie pan. Heat 2 tablespoons butter in a skillet and fry the onion until softened. Remove from the heat and add the grated cheese. Spread the mixture over the pastry shell. Mix the beaten eggs with the salt, pepper, nutmeg and cream. Pour over the onion and grated cheese and bake in a preheated 350° oven for 30 minutes. Serve hot.

Käsekrapfen

Cheese fritters

16 fritters

1 package dry yeast
½ teaspoon sugar
3 tablespoons lukewarm milk
1 to 1¼ cups flour
¼ teaspoon salt
Freshly ground black pepper
6 tablespoons grated Parmesan cheese
4 tablespoons butter
4 slices bacon, fried until crisp and crumbled
1 egg, lightly beaten

Filling:
6 tablespoons softened butter
6 ounces Camembert or Roquefort cheese
1 tablespoon finely chopped chives
1 teaspoon paprika

Sprinkle the yeast and sugar over the lukewarm milk and stir to dissolve. Let stand 10 minutes. In a large bowl combine ¼ cup flour, salt, pepper and Parmesan cheese. Cut the butter into the mixture with a pastry blender or 2 knives until it resembles coarse meal. Add the bacon, beaten egg and yeast mixture and combine thoroughly. Add the remaining flour gradually until the dough pulls away from the sides of the bowl. Turn out onto a floured board and knead until smooth and elastic, adding flour as necessary to prevent sticking. Place the dough in an oiled bowl, cover and let rise in a warm place 1 hour or until doubled in bulk. Roll the dough out as thinly as possible and cut into 32 2½ inch rounds. Place on a buttered baking sheet and bake in a 375° oven 20 minutes until golden brown. Cool on wire racks. To prepare the filling, beat the butter until smooth. Add the cheese, chives and paprika and continue beating until very well combined. Spread the bottom of each baked round with a thick layer of the cheese mixture and sandwich together in pairs. Serve with cocktails.

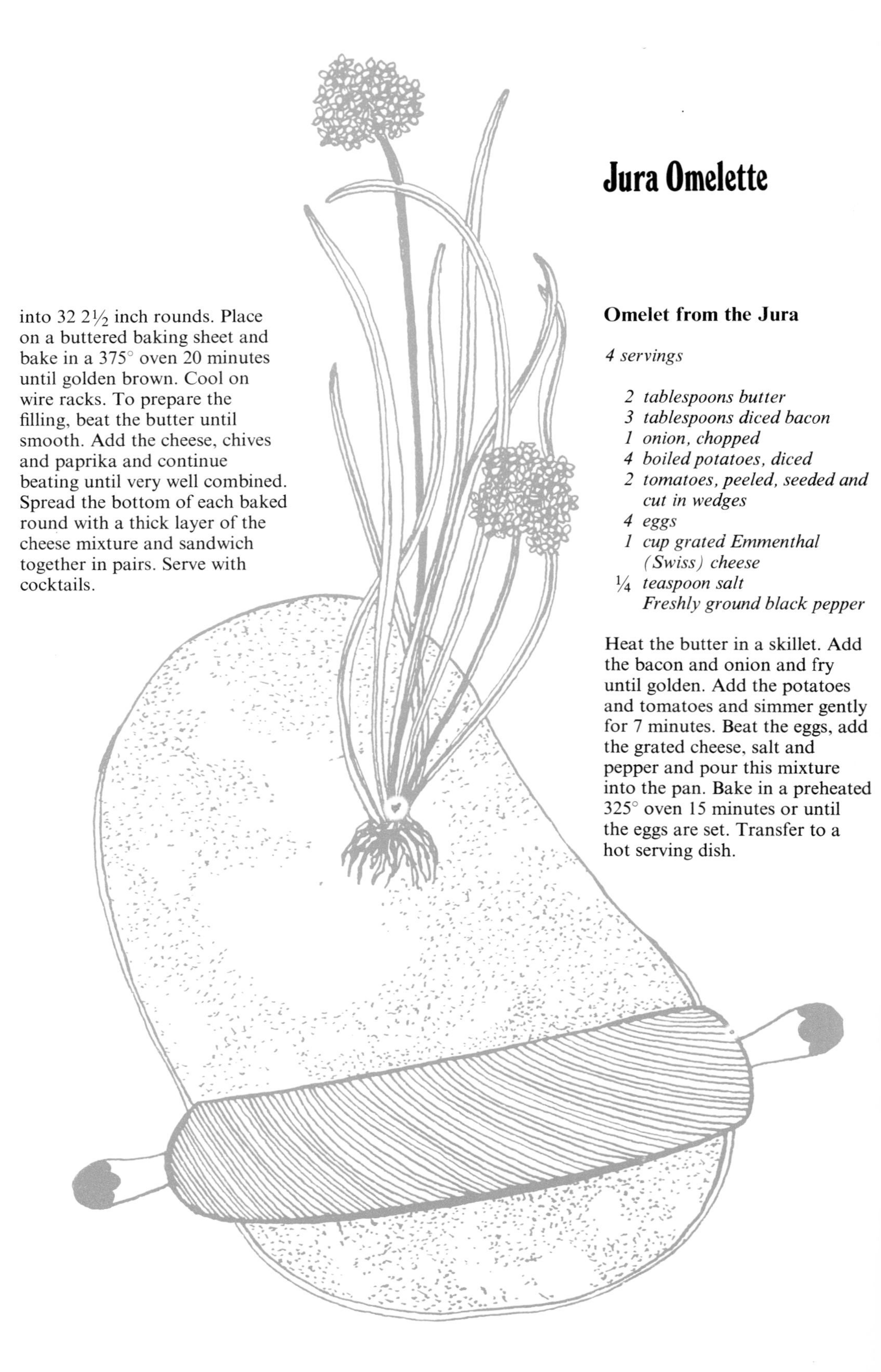

Jura Omelette

Omelet from the Jura

4 servings

2 tablespoons butter
3 tablespoons diced bacon
1 onion, chopped
4 boiled potatoes, diced
2 tomatoes, peeled, seeded and cut in wedges
4 eggs
1 cup grated Emmenthal (Swiss) cheese
¼ teaspoon salt
Freshly ground black pepper

Heat the butter in a skillet. Add the bacon and onion and fry until golden. Add the potatoes and tomatoes and simmer gently for 7 minutes. Beat the eggs, add the grated cheese, salt and pepper and pour this mixture into the pan. Bake in a preheated 325° oven 15 minutes or until the eggs are set. Transfer to a hot serving dish.

The basic ingredient in many Central European soups is a strong broth prepared with meat, beans and what Austrians call 'Mehlschwitze', flour lightly browned in lard or butter. People seldom use large quantities of green vegetables because in countries such as Switzerland and Austria winters are too long and too cold to allow much to grow. Hungarian soups are almost always red – a beautiful deep vermilion-red – which comes both from the generous amount of paprika powder sprinkled in and from the small round red peppers, 'cherry paprikas', which are fiery hot. A fire-resistant tongue is needed to eat them, and they are usually present just to add sharpness to the soup. The fiery flavor is sometimes cut by adding a few spoonfuls of thick sour cream in the individual soupbowls.
In Rumania, slightly sour soups are especially popular. They owe their fine fresh flavor to sauerkraut, one of the major ingredients. This soup not only tastes good but is also very healthy, containing large quantities of vitamin C. It relieves tiredness instantly and is perfect for 'the morning after the night before.'

Paprikás leves

Paprika soup

4 servings

½ pound bacon, diced
1 onion, coarsely chopped
2 red or green peppers, seeded and cut into thin strips
1 tablespoon flour
1 tablespoon paprika
6 cups beef broth or water
¼ teaspoon salt
4 potatoes, peeled and diced
½ cup sour cream

Fry the bacon in a large saucepan until the fat has rendered. Add the onion and peppers and continue cooking over low heat 10 minutes. Pour off all but 2 tablespoons fat. Add the flour and paprika and cook, stirring, 2 minutes. Pour in the broth gradually, stirring constantly. Add the salt and potatoes and simmer 20 minutes. Ladle into individual soup bowls and float a large spoonful of sour cream on top of the soup.

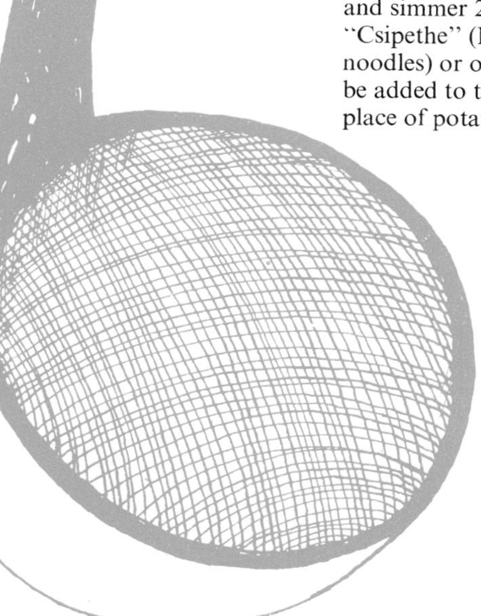

Gulyas leves

Goulash soup

6 servings

4 tablespoons butter
2 onions, coarsely chopped
1½ pounds tender beef, diced
1 tablespoon salt
1 tablespoon paprika
6 cups beef broth
1½ pounds potatoes, peeled and diced
2 tomatoes, peeled, seeded and sliced

Heat the butter in a large, heavy saucepan and sauté the onions until golden brown. Add the beef, salt, paprika and about ¼ cup broth. Lower the heat, cover and simmer 30 minutes. Add the remaining broth gradually. Cover and continue simmering for 1 hour. Add the potatoes and tomatoes and simmer 20 minutes more. "Csipethe" (Hungarian noodles) or other noodles may be added to the soup in place of potatoes.

Hühnersuppe mit Leberknödel

Chicken soup with liver dumplings

6 servings

Soup:

- *1 pound chicken giblets*
- *6 cups water*
- *1¼ teaspoons salt*
- *4 tablespoons butter*
- *2 carrots, coarsely grated*
- *1 small parsnip, coarsely grated*
- *Freshly ground black pepper*
- *1 tablespoon flour*

Dumplings:

- *2 slices white bread, soaked in water and squeezed dry*
- *½ pound chicken livers*
- *1 tablespoon chopped onion*
- *2 eggs*
- *1 teaspoon salt*
- *Freshly ground black pepper*
- *½ to ¾ cup fine dry breadcrumbs*

- *2 tablespoons sour cream*
- *1 tablespoon chopped parsley*

Place the chicken giblets, water and 1 teaspoon salt in a large pan. Bring to a boil, reduce the heat and simmer for 1¼ hours. Remove the giblets and chop finely. Heat the butter in a pan and add the carrots and parsnip. Season with the remaining salt and pepper and fry 10 to 15 minutes until softened. Stir in the flour until well blended. Add the giblet broth gradually, stirring constantly. Bring to a boil and simmer for 2 to 3 minutes. To prepare the dumplings, combine the bread, chicken livers and onion and mince or chop finely. Add the eggs, salt and pepper and enough breadcrumbs to hold the mixture together in a firm consistency. Form into 1 inch balls. Drop into the gently boiling soup and simmer for 10 minutes. Add the chopped giblets. Remove from the heat and stir in the sour cream. Serve the dumplings in the soup. Garnish with chopped parsley.

Lebersuppe mit Rahm

Creamed liver soup

4 servings

- *1 tablespoon butter*
- *¾ pound calf liver, cubed*
- *1 onion, finely chopped*
- *1 tablespoon flour*
- *4 cups beef broth*
- *1 teaspoon salt*
- *Freshly ground black pepper*
- *1 bay leaf*
- *4 tablespoons sour cream*

Heat the butter in a saucepan. Add the liver and onion and fry over moderate heat for 5 minutes. Add the flour, stirring constantly and fry for 1 minute. Add the beef broth gradually. Add the salt, pepper and bay leaf. Bring to a boil, reduce the heat, cover and simmer for 30 minutes. Remove the liver, and mince or grind it finely. Return the liver to the soup. Serve hot in individual bowls. Garnish each bowl with 1 tablespoon of sour cream.

Hálaszlé

Fish soup

4 to 6 servings

- *2 pounds whole carp, pike or other fresh water fish*
- *6 cups water*
- *1 teaspoon salt*
- *2 onions, cut into rings*
- *1 tablespoon paprika*
- *1 green pepper, seeded and cut into strips*
- *4 medium sized tomatoes, peeled, seeded and cut into wedges*
- *Freshly ground black pepper*

Have the fish cleaned and boned and cut into bite sized pieces. Reserve the trimmings. Bring 6 cups water to a boil, add salt, onions and fish trimmings. Add paprika, reduce the heat, cover and simmer for 20 minutes. Strain the broth into a clean saucepan and add the fish. Add green pepper and tomatoes and simmer for 20 minutes. Do not stir but move the pan over the flame slightly from time to time to prevent the fish from sticking to the bottom of the pan. Season to taste with black pepper.
The soup can be garnished with red or green pepper cut into rings. It may be made with 1½ pounds filleted fish and 3 cups clam broth and 3 cups water substituted for the fish broth if the trimmings are not available.

Brotsuppe mit Eiern

Bread soup with eggs

4 servings

- *1½ cups dried breadcrumbs*
- *4 cups veal broth*
- *½ teaspoon salt*
- *Freshly ground black pepper*
- *½ pound link sausage, minced*
- *1 egg yolk, lightly beaten*
- *2 hard boiled eggs, chopped*
- *1 tablespoon finely chopped parsley*

Place the breadcrumbs, broth, salt and pepper in a saucepan and set aside 20 minutes.
Bring to a boil, reduce the heat and simmer 20 minutes.
Meanwhile, fry the sausage in its own fat until nicely browned. Drain on paper towels. Strain the soup, rubbing the breadcrumbs through the sieve. Add 3 tablespoons of the broth to the egg yolk, beating constantly. Return the egg yolk mixture to the soup and add the sausage and hard boiled eggs. Stir until hot but do not allow the soup to boil. Sprinkle with parsley and serve.

Wiener Kraftsuppe

Potato soup Vienna style

6 servings

- *6 cups chicken broth or water*
- *6 potatoes, peeled and diced*
- *1 large carrot, sliced*
- *¼ teaspoon marjoram*
- *½ teaspoon caraway seeds*
- *½ teaspoon salt*
- *Freshly ground black pepper*
- *5 slices bacon, diced*
- *1 onion, finely chopped*
- *1 clove garlic, crushed*
- *4 tablespoons flour*
- *Grated rind of 1 lemon*
- *2 tablespoons finely chopped parsley*

Heat the broth to simmering point and add the potatoes, carrot, marjoram, caraway seeds, salt and pepper. Cover and simmer over low heat 20 minutes until the vegetables are tender. Meanwhile, fry the bacon until the fat has rendered. Add the onion and garlic and sauté until golden brown. Add the flour and cook, stirring, 2 minutes. Add about 1 cup of the simmering broth gradually, stirring constantly until the mixture is thick. Stir the thickened mixture into the soup and add the lemon rind. Simmer 5 minutes more. Taste for seasoning, sprinkle with parsley and serve.

Bárány leves

Lamb soup

6 servings

- *1 tablespoon oil*
- *3 onions, chopped*
- *1 tablespoon paprika*
- *2 pounds shoulder of lamb, diced*
- *1 teaspoon caraway seeds*
- *1 bay leaf*
- *1 teaspoon salt*
- *6 cups beef broth*
- *¼ pound cooked green beans*
- *4 cooked potatoes, diced*
- *1 cup sour cream*
- *2 tablespoons flour*

Heat the oil in a large saucepan and sauté the onions until golden brown. Add the paprika, lamb, caraway seeds, bay leaf and salt and just enough water to barely cover the lamb. Lower the heat, cover and simmer 1½ hours. Add the 6 cups broth, green beans and potatoes. Blend the sour cream and flour and stir into the soup. Remove from the heat before the soup boils and serve immediately.

Aargauer Spinatsuppe

Spinach soup from Aargau

6 servings

- 1/4 *pound bacon, diced*
- 2 *onions, finely chopped*
- 2 *tablespoons flour*
- 3/4 *cup milk*
- 6 *cups beef broth*
- 1 *pound fresh spinach, coarsely chopped*
- 1/4 *teaspoon salt*
- *Freshly ground black pepper*
- *Dash of nutmeg*

Fry the bacon in a large saucepan until the fat is rendered. Add the onions and continue cooking until the bacon is crisp and the onions are lightly browned. Add the flour and cook, stirring, 2 minutes. Add the milk gradually, stirring constantly until a thick sauce forms. Stir in the broth and bring to a boil. Add the spinach, salt, pepper and nutmeg. Lower the heat and simmer 12 minutes. Strain the soup, pressing down on the spinach and onions to extract all the juices. Serve in individual soup bowls and pass dishes of toasted croutons and grated Parmesan cheese separately.

Erbsensuppe mit Schweinefleisch

Pea soup with pork

4 to 6 servings

- 3/4 *pound yellow split peas*
- 1 1/2 *pounds pork butt*
- 6 *cups water*
- 1 *small onion, chopped*
- *Freshly ground black pepper*
- 1/4 *teaspoon dried marjoram*
- 5 *potatoes, peeled and cubed*

Soak the peas overnight in water. Place the pork in a large pan, add the water, bring to a boil and remove any scum. Add the onion, pepper and marjoram and simmer gently for 45 minutes. Drain and add the peas and continue cooking for another 30 minutes. Add the potatoes and simmer for 20 minutes. Remove the pork and cut it into small pieces. Return the pork to the soup. Reheat and serve.

Kabis suppe

Cabbage soup

6 servings

- 4 *tablespoons butter*
- 1 *small white cabbage, shredded*
- 1 *onion, chopped*
- 6 *cups beef broth*
- 1/4 *cup rice*
- 1 *teaspoon salt*
- *Freshly ground black pepper*
- 1/8 *teaspoon nutmeg*
- 3/4 *cup grated cheese*

Heat the butter in a saucepan. Add the cabbage and onion and sauté for 5 minutes until the cabbage is coated with butter. Add the beef broth, bring to a boil and simmer for 15 minutes. Add the rice, season with salt, pepper and nutmeg and cook for 20 minutes until the rice is tender. Place 2 tablespoons grated cheese in each individual soup bowl and pour the hot soup over it.

Houbova polevka

Mushroom soup

6 servings

- *1 small onion, finely chopped*
- *1 carrot, peeled and finely chopped*
- *6 cups veal broth*
- *2½ tablespoons butter*
- *½ pound fresh mushrooms, coarsely chopped*
- *1 tablespoon finely chopped parsley*
- *1 tablespoon flour*
- *½ teaspoon salt*
- *Freshly ground black pepper*

Place the onion, carrot and broth in a saucepan and simmer 1 hour. Heat the butter in a large saucepan and sauté the mushrooms over low heat 6 minutes. Add the parsley, cover and cook 5 minutes. Sprinkle on the flour and cook, stirring, 2 minutes. Add the broth gradually, stirring constantly. Season with salt and pepper and simmer 10 minutes more.

Kminova polevka

Caraway seed soup

6 servings

- *2 tablespoons butter*
- *1½ tablespoons flour*
- *1 tablespoon caraway seeds, lightly crushed*
- *6 cups boiling water or chicken broth*
- *1 teaspoon salt*
- *Freshly ground black pepper*
- *½ pound macaroni, cooked al dente*

Heat the butter in a large pan, add the flour and stir until lightly browned. Add the caraway seeds. Add the water gradually, stirring constantly. Reduce the heat and simmer for 40 minutes. Strain the soup and season with salt and pepper. Add the macaroni, heat and serve.

Paradiessuppe

Paradise soup

4 servings

- *2 pounds tomatoes, cut into wedges*
- *4 cups beef broth*
- *6 tablespoons butter*
- *1 onion, chopped*
- *2 tablespoons flour*
- *2 carrots, sliced*
- *¼ cup chopped celery*
- *2 cloves*
- *1 bay leaf*
- *Juice and rind of ½ lemon*
- *1 tablespoon sugar*
- *1½ teaspoons salt*
- *¾ cup cooked rice*

Simmer the tomatoes in the beef broth for 15 minutes. Strain the broth. Heat the butter in a saucepan, add the onion and fry until lightly browned. Stir in the flour gradually and add the carrots and chopped celery. Stir in the tomato broth, cloves, bay leaf, lemon juice and rind, sugar and salt. Simmer for 30 minutes. Strain. Add the cooked rice, heat thoroughly and serve.

Gurkensuppe

Cucumber soup

4 servings

- *2 tablespoons butter*
- *1 onion, finely chopped*
- *½ tablespoon finely chopped parsley*
- *1 cucumber, peeled, seeded and chopped*
- *2 tablespoons flour*
- *¾ cup heavy cream*
- *5 cups chicken broth*
- *½ teaspoon salt*
- *Freshly ground black pepper*

Heat the butter in a large saucepan and sauté the onion, parsley and cucumber over low heat until the onion is soft. Add the flour and cook, stirring, 1 minute. Add the cream and broth gradually, stirring constantly. Bring to a simmer and add salt and pepper. Serve immediately.

Bramborova polevka

Potato soup

8 servings

- *4 large potatoes, peeled and diced*
- *8 cups water*
- *1½ teaspoons salt*
- *Freshly ground black pepper*
- *1½ tablespoons butter*
- *1 carrot, coarsely grated*
- *1 tablespoon flour*
- *1 tablespoon chopped parsley*
- *½ cup milk*
- *1 egg yolk*

Place the potatoes in a saucepan. Add the water and salt and cook for 20 minutes until the potatoes are tender. Strain and reserve the cooking liquid. Mash the potatoes. Heat the butter in a pan, add the carrot and fry for 2 minutes. Reduce the heat, cover and continue cooking for 15 minutes. Stir in the flour and cook for 1 minute. Add the parsley and milk, bring to a boil and cook for 2 minutes. Add the potatoes and enough of the cooking liquid to make a creamy soup. Beat the egg yolk, stir in a few tablespoons of the soup and return to the pan, stirring until smooth. Serve hot.

Urner Käsesuppe

Cheese soup

4 servings

- *3 tablespoons butter*
- *3 tablespoons flour*
- *4 cups chicken broth*
- *1 tablespoon caraway seeds*
- *½ teaspoon salt*
- *Freshly ground black pepper*
- *Dash of nutmeg*
- *1 cup grated Emmenthal (Swiss) cheese*
- *1 cup warm milk*

Heat the butter in a large saucepan. Stir in the flour and cook over low heat until the mixture is golden brown.
Add the chicken broth gradually, stirring constantly. Add the caraway seeds, salt, pepper and nutmeg and simmer, covered, 40 minutes. Combine the cheese and milk in a soup tureen and pour in the hot soup, stirring constantly. Ladle into individual bowls.

Wiener Fleischsuppe

Beef broth with semolina dumplings

4 servings

Dumplings:

- *2 tablespoons butter*
- *1 egg*
- *¼ teaspoon salt*
- *⅛ teaspoon nutmeg*
- *6 tablespoons coarse semolina*
- *1 teaspoon cold water*
- *4 cups beef broth*
- *½ package frozen peas*
- *1 cup button mushrooms, sliced*
- *1 tablespoon chopped chives*

Cream the butter in a bowl, add the egg and season with salt and nutmeg. Mix well. Stir in the semolina and water, cover and let stand for 2 hours. Form small dumplings with a teaspoon. Bring the beef broth to a boil, lower the heat, add the dumplings and simmer for 20 minutes. Add the peas and mushrooms 10 minutes before the dumplings are cooked. Garnish with chopped chives before serving.

Kaposztaleves

Sauerkraut soup

6 servings

- *1 pound sauerkraut*
- *2 onions, cut into rings*
- *1 cup white wine*
- *4 cups beef broth*
- *½ pound ground beef*
- *½ teaspoon sugar*
- *Freshly ground black pepper*
- *2 tablespoons chopped parsley*
- *6 tablespoons yogurt*

Place the sauerkraut, onions, wine and beef broth in a saucepan. Bring to a boil and simmer for 45 minutes. Shape the ground beef into small balls, add to the soup and cook for 10 minutes. Season with sugar, pepper and parsley. Serve in individual soup bowls and garnish each serving with a tablespoon of yogurt.

Kraftbrühe mit Griesznockerl

Beef soup from Vienna

6 servings

- 2 *tablespoons butter*
- ½ *pound lean beef, diced*
- ½ *cup chopped cauliflower*
- ¾ *cup shredded cabbage*
- 1 *tablespoon chopped celery leaves*
- 1 *onion, finely chopped*
- ¼ *pound mushrooms, sliced*
- 4 *cups beef broth*
- ½ *teaspoon salt*
- *Freshly ground black pepper*
- 1 *tablespoon finely chopped parsley*
- ½ *cup toasted croutons*

Heat the butter in a large saucepan. Add the beef, cauliflower, cabbage, celery leaves, onion and mushrooms and sauté over medium heat 2 minutes. Reduce the heat, cover and cook 8 minutes. Add the broth, bring to a boil and skim. Add the salt and pepper, reduce the heat, cover and cook 10 minutes more. Ladle into individual soup bowls, sprinkle with parsley and croutons and serve.

Beef broth with semolina dumplings.
In Hungary the hostess serves spicy, slightly sour, sauerkraut soup at the end of a party. This probably gives the guests the energy and courage to face the ride home. Sauerkraut does actually have a high vitamin C content (recipe page 24, 4th column).

Dumplings

Austrian cooking would be much the poorer without its small dumplings, tiny balls made of flour, potatoes and bread and mixed with meat or filled with fruit. These 'knödel' and 'gnockerl' are almost never missing from an Austrian meal. When you first go to Austria and have a bowl of soup set before you, you might ask yourself why so much trouble was taken to make a dumpling when they could have just dropped a baked potato in the soup. But the knödel is very different from a simple potato-quite a unique experience. Knödel, gnockerl and all the other potato, flour and bread balls are absolutely indispensable to Austrian cooking. A particular treat is soup with a good 'Leberknödel', a liver knödel which must be carefully broken in the broth. Other varieties of knödel only come into their own when the apricots ripen in July along the Danube. This is the time for tasting a hot Marillenknödel, filled with fresh, juicy apricots whose pits have been filled with lumps of sugar soaked in Marillenbrand, a delicious apricot brandy. During the apricot festival held every year in Wachau thousands of these knödel are washed down with giant glasses of delightful white Wachauer wine.

Nudelteig

Plain noodle dough

2 cups flour
1 teaspoon salt
2 eggs
¼ cup water

Sift the flour and salt together onto a pastry board. Beat the eggs lightly, and add the water gradually. Make a well in the center of the flour and pour in about ½ the liquid ingredients. Work the flour into the liquid with your fingertips adding more liquid gradually until it is all used. Knead the dough several minutes until very smooth. Roll it out as thinly as possible and let stand to dry out slightly. Roll the dough up like a jelly roll and cut into thin strips. Let the strips dry 30 minutes before cooking.

Semmelknödel

Bread dumplings

6 servings

2 tablespoons butter
2 teaspoons chopped parsley
1 cup fresh breadcrumbs
1 tablespoon milk
2 eggs, separated
½ teaspoon salt
Pinch of white pepper
⅛ teaspoon ground marjoram
4 tablespoons flour
2 cups chicken broth or salted water

Heat the butter in a saucepan, add the parsley and fry gently for 2 minutes. Place the breadcrumbs in a bowl and add the milk. Stir in the beaten egg yolks, salt, pepper, marjoram and fried parsley. Beat the egg whites until stiff and fold into the breadcrumb mixture. Form small dumplings with a spoon and dredge in flour. Drop into simmering chicken broth or salted water and poach the dumplings for 20 minutes.

Kartoffelknödel

Potato dumplings

3 large potatoes, cooked, peeled and mashed
1½ cups cooked rice
1½ tablespoons melted butter
3 heaping tablespoons diced cooked ham
2 teaspoons finely chopped parsley
2 egg yolks, beaten
½ teaspoon salt
Freshly ground black pepper
Oil for deep frying

Place all the ingredients except the oil in a bowl and combine thoroughly. Lightly flour your hands and form the mixture into small balls. Heat the oil for deep frying and fry the dumplings a few at a time until golden brown. Drain on paper towels and serve.

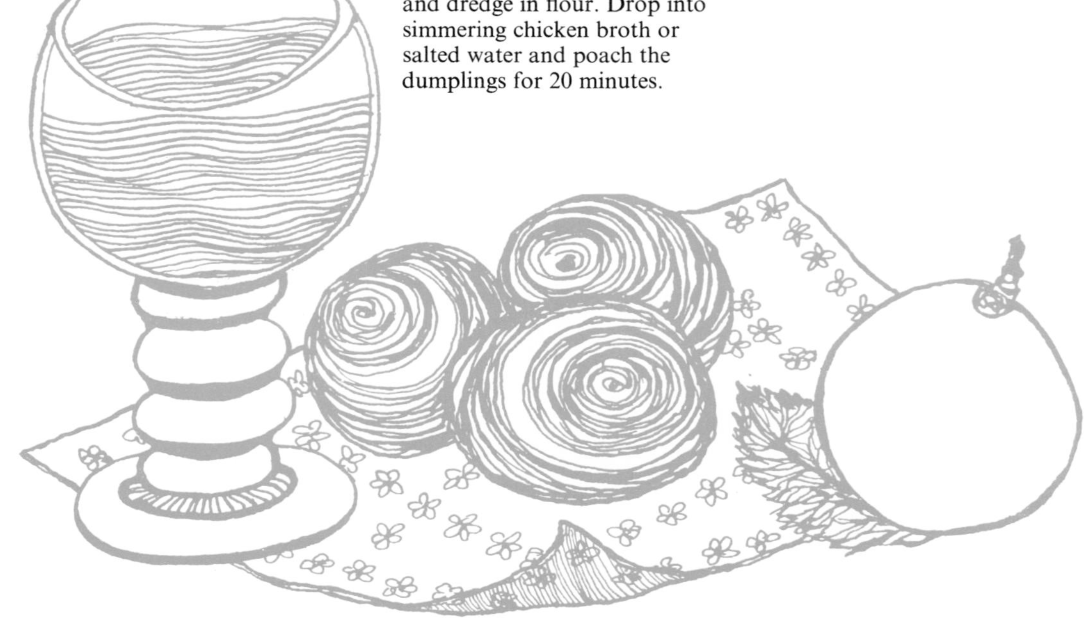

Leberknödel

Liver dumplings

6 to 8 servings

3 tablespoons butter
1 large onion, finely chopped
2 tablespoons chopped parsley
2 pounds calves' liver, ground
1½ teaspoons salt
Freshly ground black pepper
⅛ teaspoon marjoram
1½ cups water
2½ cups dried breadcrumbs
3 eggs, beaten

Heat the butter, add the onion and fry 2 minutes. Add the parsley and fry 1 minute. Add the liver, salt, pepper and marjoram and continue cooking for 5 minutes, stirring occasionally. Heat the water in a saucepan, add the breadcrumbs and cook for 3 minutes. Combine the liver mixture and breadcrumbs and add the beaten eggs. Stir until well blended. Shape the mixture into walnut sized balls and simmer gently in boiling, salted water for 20 to 25 minutes or until they are tender. Serve with chicken soup. Dumplings may be simmered directly in the soup in which they are to be served.

Schinkenfleckern

Ham patches

4 servings

1 recipe noodle dough (page 26)
4 tablespoons butter
½ cup heavy cream
3 eggs
1 cup minced cooked ham
¼ teaspoon salt
Freshly ground black pepper
1 tablespoon butter
¼ cup dry breadcrumbs

Roll the dough out ¼ inch thick and cut into 2 inch squares. Cook in plenty of boiling salted water for 10 to 15 minutes or until barely tender. Rinse under cold running water until the noodles are completely cooled. Drain thoroughly. Heat the butter in a large skillet and toss the noodles with the butter until lightly browned. Beat the cream until fluffy. Beat the eggs separately until thick and fold into the cream. Add the noodles, ham, salt and pepper and combine gently but thoroughly. Butter an ovenproof casserole and sprinkle with breadcrumbs. Pour in the noodle mixture and bake in a 325° oven for 50 minutes. Serve from the casserole.

Aargauer Kartoffelpfluten

Potato dumplings, Aargau style

4 servings

6 medium sized potatoes, peeled and boiled
2 eggs
1 teaspoon salt
Freshly ground black pepper
⅛ teaspoon ground nutmeg
½ cup flour
¾ cup grated Swiss cheese
6 tablespoons butter
1 onion, cut into rings
6 tablespoons fine breadcrumbs

Mash or rice the potatoes and add the eggs, salt, pepper, nutmeg, flour and ½ the grated cheese. Beat until smooth. Form the mixture into 1 inch balls. Drop into gently boiling, salted water and simmer for 10 minutes. Drain the dumplings and place in a flat dish. Keep the dumplings warm. Melt the butter, add the onion rings and sauté for 5 minutes. Sprinkle dumplings with breadcrumbs and the remaining cheese. Top with onion rings and the hot cooking butter. Serve with a fresh green salad.

Nudelschöberl

Noodle pie

4 servings

1 recipe noodle dough (page 26)
4 cups milk
3 eggs, separated
3 tablespoons butter, softened
½ teaspoon salt
Freshly ground black pepper

Roll the dough out ¼ inch thick and cut into 1 inch squares. Bring the milk to a boil and add the noodle squares. Cook 10 to 15 minutes until tender. Remove the pan from the heat and let the noodles cool in the milk. Stir occasionally to prevent sticking. Beat the egg yolks with the butter until creamy. Drain the noodles and add to the egg yolk/butter mixture. Stir in the salt and pepper. Beat the egg whites until stiff. Stir in ⅓ of the egg whites and gently fold in the remainder. Spoon into a buttered pie plate or shallow ovenproof casserole and bake in a 325° oven 45 minutes until golden brown. Cut into wedges and serve with soup or grilled meat.

Fish dishes

In all small fishing villages along the Danube in Hungary, the fishermen cook the traditional carp soup in iron pots over an open reed fire. The soup must be fiery red and hot from paprika.

Ponty leves

Carp soup

4 to 6 servings

- 3 *pounds carp or other fresh water fish, filleted*
- 6 *cups water*
- 3 *onions, cut into rings*
- 1 *tablespoon paprika*
- 1 *teaspoon salt*
- *Freshly ground black pepper*

Cut the fish into thick slices. Place the fish heads, bones and trimmings in a saucepan. Add the water, onions, paprika, salt and pepper. Cover and simmer for 1 hour. Strain the broth into a clean saucepan. Add the fish slices and simmer for 25 minutes. The soup may be served immediately or chilled and served cold as a jellied soup.
Note: It is necessary to use fish trimmings to make the broth for this soup. The bones will cause the broth to jell when it cools.

Carp is the great fish of the Donau, and carp prepared in a piquant paprika sauce is the crowning pride of any good Hungarian restaurant.

Paprika Karpfen

Paprika carp

4 servings

- *3 tablespoons butter*
- *2 onions, finely chopped*
- *1 clove garlic, crushed*
- *2 teaspoons paprika*
- *1 green pepper, seeded and chopped*
- *1 (2 to 3 pound) carp, cleaned and cut into pieces*
- *½ teaspoon salt*
- *Freshly ground black pepper*
- *1 tablespoon chopped parsley*
- *¼ cup white wine*
- *2 tablespoons tomato paste*

Heat the butter in a casserole and fry the onions and garlic until soft and golden. Add the paprika and green pepper and fry for 5 minutes. Add the fish and season with salt, pepper and chopped parsley. Add the wine and stir in the tomato paste. Simmer gently for about 15 minutes until the fish is tender and flakes easily. Add a little water during cooking if necessary.

Central Europe lies far from the sea, but its broad rivers and magnificent lakes yield great quantities of fish. Choice varieties of trout come from the mountain streams of Switzerland, Austria and even Czechoslovakia. These fish taste best when simply boiled with some vinegar and fresh herbs and eaten with masses of melted butter. Mighty perch swim in the lakes of Switzerland, Austria and Hungary, and though these all belong to the same family, each lake has its own special variety, such as the 'omble chevalier' from Lake Geneva or the 'fogas' from Hungary's Lake Balaton. Fortunately, delicious full-flavored white wines grow on the sunny hillsides around the lakes, and these wines form the perfect complement to perch. But the king of freshwater fish is the carp that swims in the Danube and its tributaries. In Austria, cold carp in a slightly sour wine jelly is the traditional dish on Christmas Eve. Hungarian carp is prepared to perfection in the small fishing villages along the Danube. The very best comes from Aunt Juliska's in Kálocsa, where you can sit behind her house under the nut trees by the Danube. There you can see how Aunt Juliska, dressed in her long wide skirt and wearing her bordered head scarf, transforms the carp that just a few hours earlier had been swimming in the river.
Carp soup and carp stew are a fiery red from paprika, and so hot that you gasp for breath after the first bite. But by the third mouthful you have already become accustomed to the taste, especially if there is a handy pitcher of white wine to extinguish the flames.

Karpf im Rotwein

Carp in red wine

4 servings

- *1 (2 to 2½ pound) fresh carp*
- *2 cups dry red wine*
- *1 bay leaf*
- *8 peppercorns*
- *½ teaspoon thyme*
- *2 sprigs parsley*
- *½ teaspoon salt*
- *Freshly ground black pepper*
- *½ cup button mushrooms*
- *2 tablespoons butter*
- *2 teaspoons flour*

Clean and scale the fish and score crosswise as deep as the bone. Place in a large saucepan with the wine, bay leaf, peppercorns, thyme and parsley. Season with salt and pepper and add the mushrooms. Bring to simmering point. Cover and simmer gently for 12 minutes until the fish flakes easily. Transfer the fish carefully to a serving dish and keep warm. Strain the liquid. Heat the butter in a saucepan, stir in the flour and continue stirring until the flour is a golden brown. Add the strained liquid gradually. Stir with a wire whisk to form a smooth sauce. Pour the sauce over the fish and serve immediately.

Pontypörkölt

Carp stew

4 to 6 servings

- *1 (4 to 6 pound) carp*
- *1 teaspoon salt*
- *2 cups water*
- *2 tablespoons paprika*
- *3 tablespoons butter*
- *4 onions, sliced into thin rings*
- *2 green peppers, seeded and sliced into thin rings*
- *4 tomatoes, peeled, seeded and sliced*

Have the fish man clean the carp and cut it into large pieces. Reserve the head, tail and bones. Sprinkle the pieces of fish with ½ teaspoon salt and set aside. Bring the water to a boil and add the remaining salt, paprika and reserved fish trimmings. Lower the heat and simmer 20 to 30 minutes. Meanwhile, heat the butter and sauté the onions until golden brown. Arrange the fish in a buttered heatproof casserole and place the onions, peppers and tomatoes on top. Strain the broth over the fish and vegetables. Cover and simmer 15 to 20 minutes until the fish flakes easily with a fork. Serve with potatoes or noodles.

Karpfen mit saurer Sahne

Carp with sour cream

6 servings

6 carp fillets
1 teaspoon salt
Freshly ground black pepper
⅔ cup dry white wine
¾ cup sliced mushrooms
1 onion, chopped
2 tablespoons chopped parsley
⅓ cup water
2 tablespoons butter
2 tablespoons flour
½ cup sour cream
½ cup whipping cream

Sprinkle the fish with salt and pepper. Place in a casserole and add the wine. Cover with mushrooms, onion and parsley. Add the water and bring to a boil. Cover, reduce the heat and simmer 20 minutes. Drain and reserve the broth from the fish. Place the fish and mushrooms on a heated serving dish. Heat the butter in a pan, stir in the flour and cook over low heat for 1 minute. Add the fish broth and continue cooking until the sauce has thickened. Stir in the sour cream and whipped cream and reheat. Pour the sauce over the fish and serve with boiled potatoes.

Kapr na cerno

Carp in black sauce

6 servings

2 tablespoons butter
1 small onion, finely chopped
½ cup diced celery
½ cup diced carrots
½ cup diced parsnips
½ teaspoon salt
8 peppercorns
1 bay leaf
1 tablespoon thyme
2 tablespoons water
½ cup beer
Juice and grated rind of 1 lemon
3 tablespoons wine vinegar
½ cup red wine
2 teaspoons sugar
¼ cup chopped walnuts
6 pitted prunes, chopped
¼ cup raisins
2 tablespoons plum preserves or blackberry jelly
6 thick slices carp
2 tablespoons chopped blanched almonds

Heat the butter in a saucepan and sauté the onions, celery, carrots and parsnips over moderate heat until softened. Add the salt, peppercorns, bay leaf, thyme and water. Cover and simmer over very low heat 20 minutes. Purée the mixture in a blender and force through a sieve into a casserole. Add the beer, lemon juice and rind, vinegar, wine, sugar, walnuts, prunes, raisins and preserves. Bring to a boil, reduce the heat and add the carp. Cover and simmer 12 to 15 minutes until the fish flakes easily with a fork. Carefully transfer the fish slices to a heated serving dish and pour over the sauce. Sprinkle with almonds and serve.

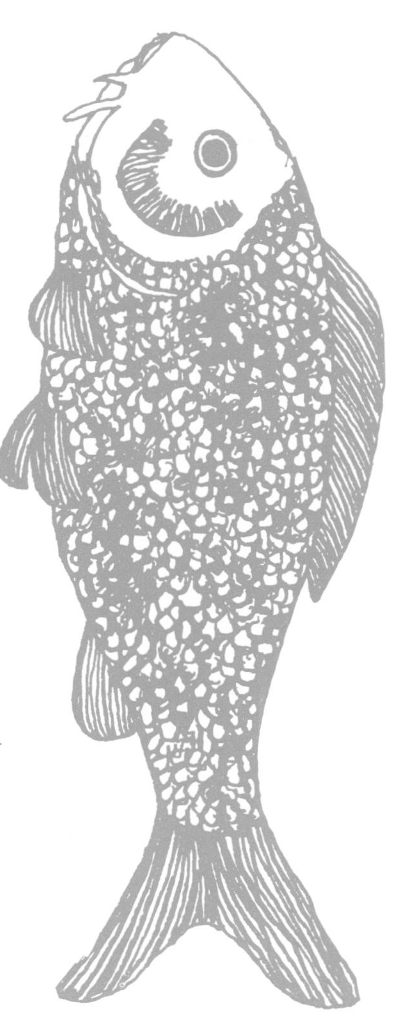

Lachs nach Basler Art

Salmon Basler style

4 servings

2 pounds salmon, cut in 1 inch thick slices
½ teaspoon salt
Freshly ground black pepper
Juice of 1 lemon
¼ cup flour
2 tablespoons butter
2 tablespoons oil
2 onions, thinly sliced into rings
¼ cup dry white wine
1 tablespoon finely chopped parsley
1 lemon, thinly sliced

Sprinkle the salmon slices on both sides with salt, pepper and lemon juice. Dredge in flour and pat off the excess. Heat the butter and oil in a large skillet and sauté the onions over medium heat until golden brown. Remove from the pan with a slotted spoon and keep warm. Raise the heat under the skillet and sauté the salmon quickly, about 2 minutes on each side. Do not overcook. Transfer the salmon to a heated platter and arrange the onion rings on top. Pour the wine into the skillet and scrape up the brown bits clinging to the pan. Pour the pan juices over the salmon, garnish with parsley and lemon slices and serve.

Fried carp is the traditional dish eaten on Christmas Eve in Austria; meat is never served on this night.

Trout with tomato and bacon *(recipe page 34, 2nd column).*

Gebackener Karpfen

Fried carp

4 servings

- 4 *fillets of carp or other fresh water fish*
- 1 *teaspoon salt*
- *Freshly ground black pepper*
- 1 *tablespoon flour*
- 1 *egg*
- 1 *tablespoon water*
- ½ *cup fine dry breadcrumbs*
- 6 *tablespoons butter*
- 1 *lemon, sliced*
- 1 *tablespoon chopped parsley*

Season the fillets of fish with salt and pepper and dust with flour. Beat the egg and water together. Dip the fillets in the egg and water mixture and then into the breadcrumbs. Heat the butter, add the fish and fry 5 minutes on each side until golden. Transfer to a serving dish. Garnish with slices of lemon and parsley. Serve with a salad and dumplings.

Ticino is the southernmost canton of Switzerland, and here the sun and the food is somewhat Italian. This salmon dish prepared with grated cheese and tomato sauce is a Swiss-Italian mixture.

Salmone alla ticinese

Salmon Ticino style

4 servings

- *4 ($\frac{1}{2}$ pound) salmon steaks*
- *$\frac{1}{2}$ teaspoon salt*
- *$\frac{1}{4}$ cup grated Emmenthal (Swiss) cheese*
- *1 tablespoon flour*
- *$\frac{1}{2}$ cup sour cream*
- *Freshly ground black pepper*
- *Dash of nutmeg*
- *4 tablespoons oil*
- *1 lemon, thinly sliced*
- *Sprigs of parsley*

Sprinkle the salmon steaks on both sides with salt. In a small bowl, combine the cheese, flour, sour cream, pepper and nutmeg. Heat the oil in a skillet and sauté the salmon steaks over high heat about 30 seconds on each side. Arrange the steaks in a buttered casserole and spoon the sauce over. Bake in a 375° oven 10 to 15 minutes. Garnish with lemon slices and parsley sprigs and serve from the casserole. Tomato sauce can be served separately.

Kalte Forellenfilets

Cold trout

4 servings

- *4 small trout, cleaned*
- *1 hard boiled egg, sliced*
- *½ cup green beans, cooked and finely chopped*
- *1 black truffle, finely chopped (optional)*
- *Aspic (recipe page 14)*
- *½ cup mayonnaise*

Bring fish broth or salted water to a simmer in a shallow saucepan and add the trout. Reduce the heat, cover and simmer about 4 minutes. Carefully remove the trout from the liquid and let cool. Fillet the trout and remove the skin, leaving a ½ to 1 inch strip down the center. Arrange the fillets on a flat serving dish and decorate with sliced egg, green beans and trufflles. Prepare the aspic as indicated on page 14 and spoon several layers of the syrupy liquid over the fillets, chilling the fish between each layer. Serve cold with mayonnaise.

Forellen mit Paradiesäpfeln

Trout with tomato and bacon

4 servings

- *4 small trout*
- *8 thin slices bacon*
- *3 tablespoons butter*
- *1½ tablespoons flour*
- *1 cup hot milk*
- *¼ teaspoon salt*
- *Freshly ground black pepper*
- *6 tomatoes peeled, seeded and finely chopped*
- *½ tablespoon finely chopped parsley*

Clean the trout and wrap each in 2 slices of bacon. Place in an oiled shallow casserole and bake in a 350° oven for 15 minutes. Meanwhile, heat 2 tablespoons butter in a saucepan. Add the flour and cook, stirring, 1 minute. Add the milk gradually, stirring until the sauce thickens. Season with salt and pepper. Force the chopped tomatoes through a strainer and cook them in the remaining butter for 5 minutes, stirring constantly. Add the tomatoes to the sauce and simmer 2 to 3 minutes. Remove the bacon from the trout and arrange the fish on a platter. Pour the sauce over, garnish with parsley and serve.

Tiroler Forellen

Tyrolean trout

4 servings

- *1 tablespoon chopped parsley*
- *1 tablespoon chopped chives*
- *2 tablespoons capers, drained*
- *2 dill pickles, chopped*
- *1 cup mayonnaise*
- *2 pounds trout fillets*
- *1 teaspoon salt*
- *Freshly ground black pepper*
- *4 tablespoons flour*
- *4 tablespoons butter*
- *1 lemon, thinly sliced*

Stir the parsley, chives, capers and pickles into the mayonnaise. Chill in the refrigerator for 2 hours. Wash the trout fillets and pat dry. Sprinkle with salt and pepper and dredge in flour. Heat the butter in a large skillet, add the fish and fry 3 minutes on each side, until golden brown. Transfer to a hot serving dish, garnish with lemon slices and serve. Pass the cold sauce separately.

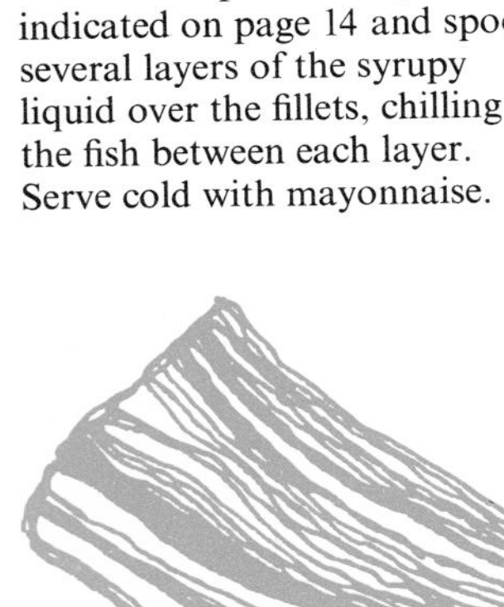

Fischfilets nach Wiener Art

Stuffed fillets Vienna style

4 servings

- *4 (½ pound) fish fillets*
- *¼ teaspoon salt*
- *Juice of 1 lemon*
- *½ cup sour cream*
- *3 slices bacon, diced*
- *4 gherkins, chopped*
- *1 tablespoon chopped capers*
- *1 tablespoon mild (Dijon type) mustard*
- *4 tablespoons grated Parmesan cheese*
- *1 tablespoon butter*

Sprinkle the fish fillets with salt and lemon juice. Place 1 fillet in a buttered casserole. Spread 2 tablespoons sour cream on the fillet and sprinkle with ¼ of the bacon, ¼ of the gherkins and ¼ of the capers. Brush another fillet with ⅓ of the mustard and place on top of the first. Spread the second with sour cream and sprinkle with bacon, gherkin and capers. Repeat these steps with the 2 remaining fillets. Sprinkle the cheese on top and dot with butter. Bake in a 350° oven for 25 to 30 minutes. Transfer to a heated serving plate, slice and serve.

Gefüllter Hecht

Stuffed pike or perch

4 servings

- *1 (5 pound) pike or perch*
- *3 cups water*
- *½ teaspoon salt*
- *1 tablespoon vinegar*
- *4 peppercorns, crushed*
- *¼ teaspoon thyme*
- *1 onion, sliced*
- *4 slices bread, crusts removed*
- *½ cup milk*
- *4 anchovy fillets, chopped*
- *1 egg*
- *Dash of nutmeg*
- *3 tablespoons butter*
- *½ cup sliced mushrooms*
- *3 tablespoons flour*
- *1 tablespoon tomato purée*

Have the fish man clean the fish and remove the head, tail and fins. Reserve the trimmings. Bring the water to a boil and add the reserved fish trimmings, salt, vinegar, peppercorns, thyme and onion. Lower the heat and simmer 20 to 30 minutes. Strain and reserve the broth. Flake any pieces of flesh on the head and tail and place in a bowl. Soak the bread in the milk. Squeeze out the excess milk and crumble the bread into the bowl. Add the anchovies, egg and nutmeg and combine thoroughly. Spread the mixture in the cavity of the fish and wrap in oiled aluminum foil. Bake in a 375° oven 35 minutes. In the meantime, heat the butter in a saucepan and sauté the mushrooms over high heat, stirring constantly for 2 or 3 minutes. Stir in the flour and cook 1 minute. Add the tomato purée and 2 cups of the reserved broth gradually, stirring constantly until the sauce has thickened. Transfer the fish to a heated platter and place the sauce in a serving bowl. Serve with parslied potatoes.

Hecht in Kapernsauce

Pike in caper sauce

4 servings

- *4 fillets of pike (about 2 pounds)*
- *1 teaspoon salt*
- *Freshly ground black pepper*
- *1 tablespoon lemon juice*
- *4 tablespoons flour*
- *6 tablespoons butter*
- *1 tablespoon mild prepared mustard*
- *2 tablespoons capers*
- *½ cup white wine*
- *¼ cup heavy cream*
- *1 teaspoon cornstarch dissolved in 1 tablespoon cold water*

Season the fish on both sides with salt and pepper. Sprinkle with lemon juice and dredge in flour. Heat the butter in a skillet and fry the fish 4 to 5 minutes on each side until golden brown. Transfer to a warm serving dish. Reheat the butter used for frying the fish and stir in the mustard, capers, white wine and cream. If desired, stir in the cornstarch to thicken the sauce. Pour the sauce over the fish and serve with a crisp green salad and bread.

Sea fish are rarely eaten in Central Europe, but freshwater fish is available in great abundance. The Austrians often eat pike in a delicious caper sauce, but they have also learned from the Hungarians to stew it in a tomato and paprika sauce.

Pike in caper sauce (recipe page 35, 4th column).

Fischragout

Fish stew

4 servings

1 pound filleted fish (swordfish or striped bass)
4 cups water
1 tablespoon wine vinegar
1 bay leaf
4 crushed peppercorns
¼ pound bacon, diced
1 onion, chopped
2 tablespoons tomato purée
1 small green pepper, cut in thin strips
½ teaspoon salt
Freshly ground black pepper
1 teaspoon paprika

Cut the fish into 2 inch pieces. Bring the water, vinegar, bay leaf and peppercorns to boiling point. Add the fish, reduce the heat and simmer for 10 minutes. Fry the bacon until the fat has rendered. Add the onion and cook 5 minutes until soft and golden. Add 1 cup of the fish broth, tomato purée, green pepper, salt and pepper and simmer for 10 minutes. Add the paprika and fish and simmer for 5 minutes. Serve immediately.

German influence can be tasted very strongly in much Czechoslovakian cooking. This marinated herring in cream sauce is an example, (recipe page 38, 1st column).

Heringe Böhmer Art

Herring fillets Bohemian style

4 servings

- *8 salted herring*
- *1½ cups water*
- *½ cup wine vinegar*
- *2 bay leaves*
- *6 peppercorns, crushed*
- *2 tablespoons chopped parsley*
- *1 stalk celery, chopped*
- *2 carrots, sliced*
- *2 onions, cut into rings*
- *1 cup milk or cream*
- *Grated rind of 1 lemon*
- *2 teaspoons capers*

Soak the herring in water for 3 hours. Bring the water and vinegar to a boil. Add the bay leaves, peppercorns, parsley, celery and carrots. Simmer for 20 minutes. Drain the herring and arrange in a dish. Cover with onion rings. Add the milk or cream to the marinade and pour over the herrings. Finally add the lemon rind and capers. Cover and refrigerate for 6 days.

Hal keszthely

Pike or perch Keszthely

4 servings

- *4 whole (¾ pound) pike or perch*
- *1 teaspoon salt*
- *1 tablespoon paprika*
- *4 tablespoons butter*
- *4 large cooked potatoes, sliced*
- *1 cup whipping cream*
- *2 tablespoons chopped parsley*

Make incisions in the skin of the fish and rub with salt and paprika. Place the fish in a buttered baking dish. Add the remaining butter. Bake in a preheated 375° oven for 8 minutes until half done. Arrange the sliced potatoes around the fish and bake for another 8 minutes or until the fish is tender. Pour the cream over the fish and heat the cream to the simmering point. Arrange the potatoes on a warm serving dish, place the fish on top of the potatoes and pour over the pan juices. Garnish with chopped parsley.

Hal gombaval

Fish and mushrooms

4 servings

- *4 medium sized potatoes, peeled and cut in half*
- *1½ pounds white fish fillets*
- *½ teaspoon salt*
- *Freshly ground black pepper*
- *⅓ cup flour*
- *¼ pound mushrooms, finely chopped*
- *1 tablespoon finely chopped parsley*
- *1 tablespoon flour*
- *¼ cup heavy cream*
- *1 cup chicken broth*
- *Juice of ½ lemon*

Place the potatoes in a pan and add cold salted water to cover. Place the lid on the pan, bring to a boil and cook 12 to 15 minutes until the potatoes are almost tender. Drain and set aside. Sprinkle the fish fillets on both sides with salt and pepper and dredge in flour. Arrange in a buttered ovenproof casserole and surround with the potatoes. Sprinkle the mushrooms and parsley on top. In a bowl, combine the flour and cream until the mixture is smooth. Add the broth and lemon juice, beating constantly with a wire whisk. Pour into the casserole and bake in a 350° oven 8 minutes. Reduce the heat to 300° and bake 25 minutes more. Serve from the casserole.

Fisch mit Spargeln

Fish with asparagus

4 servings

- 1 *(3 pound) whole firm fleshed white fish such as haddock*
- *Water*
- 1 *teaspoon salt*
- *Freshly ground black pepper*
- 1 *small onion, coarsely chopped*
- *Few sprigs parsley*
- 3 *tablespoons butter*
- 2 *tablespoons flour*
- ½ *cup milk*
- 10 *to 12 asparagus spears, cut into 1 inch pieces and cooked until tender*
- 1 *egg yolk, beaten*
- 3 *tablespoons grated Parmesan cheese*
- 2 *tablespoons breadcrumbs*

Place the fish in a fish poacher or roasting pan and add water to cover. Add salt, pepper, onion and parsley and bring to a boil. Lower the heat and simmer 10 to 12 minutes. Carefully remove the fish, drain and place in a buttered shallow ovenproof serving dish. Strain the broth into a saucepan and boil over high heat until reduced to 1 cup. Heat 2 tablespoons of the butter in another saucepan. Stir in the flour and cook 1 minute. Gradually add the reduced broth and milk, stirring constantly until the sauce is thickened and smooth. Add the asparagus, taste for seasoning and remove from the heat. Stir in the egg yolk and cheese and pour the sauce over the fish. Sprinkle with breadcrumbs and dot with the remaining butter. Bake in a 350° oven 8 to 10 minutes until golden brown.

Schollenschnitzel

Flounder fillets

4 servings

- 4 *fillets of flounder*
- ½ *teaspoon salt*
- *Freshly ground black pepper*
- 4 *tablespoons butter*
- 1 *tablespoon chopped shallots or scallions*
- 1 *tablespoon chopped parsley*
- 1 *tablespoon flour*
- 1 *anchovy, washed, dried and minced*
- ¼ *cup clam juice*
- ¼ *cup water*
- *Juice of ½ lemon*

Wash and dry the fish and sprinkle with salt and pepper. Heat the butter in a skillet, add the shallots and fry gently for 2 minutes. Add the parsley and fry for 1 minute over low heat. Increase the heat and add the fish. Fry the fish 4 to 5 minutes on each side until golden brown. Transfer to a heated serving dish. Stir the flour into the pan until well blended and add the anchovy, clam juice, water and lemon juice. Stir and cook until thickened. Pour the sauce over the fish and serve.

Peste al bastru

Fish in foil

4 servings

- 4 *whole red mullets*
- 1 *teaspoon salt*
- *Freshly ground black pepper*
- 3 *to 4 tablespoons oil*
- 8 *thin slices lemon*
- 2 *tablespoons chopped chives*
- 1 *tablespoon chopped parsley*
- 2 *tablespoons butter*

The fish should be cleaned and scaled, but left whole. Pat dry with a clean cloth and make a few incisions along the side of the fish. Rub salt and pepper into the skin. Cut 4 pieces of aluminum foil large enough to enclose each fish entirely. Brush the foil with a little oil, place the fish in the center and brush the fish with oil. Garnish with lemon slices, chives, parsley and small pats of butter. Fold the foil over the fish and seal into a neat package. Place the fish on an oven rack in a preheated 350° oven and bake for 35 minutes. Serve as a package on individual plates.

Goulash with pickled cucumbers

Goulash is Hungarian in origin, but all the countries surrounding Hungary, including Austria, have adopted this dish.

The best features of Central European cooking can be tasted in those dishes which are slowly simmered, such as meat stews or stewed pork and rice, (recipe page 42, 3rd column).

Znaimer Goulasch

Goulash with pickled cucumbers

6 servings

2½ to 3 pounds rump steak, cut into 2 inch cubes
½ cup flour seasoned with ½ teaspoon salt
Freshly ground black pepper
2 tablespoons butter
2 tablespoons oil
6 onions, coarsely chopped
1 tablespoon paprika
2 cups beef broth
3 tablespoons tomato purée
½ teaspoon marjoram
¼ teaspoon caraway seeds
1 clove garlic, crushed
Grated rind of 1 lemon
Pickled cucumbers
Boiled potatoes

Dredge the cubes of meat in seasoned flour and sauté over high heat in the hot combined butter and oil until nicely browned on all sides. Transfer to a casserole with a slotted spoon. Add the onions to the butter and oil and sauté over medium heat until golden brown. Add paprika, ½ cup broth, tomato purée, marjoram, caraway seeds, garlic and lemon rind and simmer 3 minutes. Add the remaining broth and pour over the meat in the casserole. Bring to a simmer, cover and cook slowly 1½ hours or until the meat is tender. Serve from the casserole and pass bowls of pickled cucumbers and boiled potatoes separately.

Gulyas

Goulash

6 servings

2 pounds sirloin steak, cut into 1 inch cubes
1 teaspoon salt
Freshly ground black pepper
3 tablespoons butter
4 onions, coarsely chopped
2 cups beef broth or water
4 medium sized potatoes, peeled and cubed
1 clove garlic, crushed
1 teaspoon caraway seeds
1 tablespoon paprika
2 green peppers, seeded and cut into rings
4 medium sized tomatoes, peeled, seeded and sliced

Season the beef with salt and pepper. Heat the butter and fry the onions until soft and golden. Add the beef and fry over high heat for 5 minutes until browned on all sides. Add the beef broth, cover and simmer for 1¼ hours. Add the potatoes, garlic and caraway seeds and sprinkle with paprika. Arrange the peppers and tomatoes on top. Cover and continue cooking for 25 minutes until the vegetables are tender. In Hungary, goulash is served with "scipethe," flake-formed pasta, for which wide noodles can be substituted.

The Hungarian word 'gulyás' means cow herder, and goulash, the dish prepared with meat, onions and paprika that has become famous throughout the world, has been for centuries the traditional meal of the cattlemen on the wide Hungarian plains. When the sun goes down and the cattle have been watered, a fire is built beside the whitewashed cabin of the cattlemen. Over the flames stands a tripod holding a heavy iron pot in which the 'gulyás' is cooked. This classical 'gulyás' is called 'bográcsgulyás', kettle goulash, and in most restaurants it is served from an iron pot at the table. This traditional goulash is more a kind of soup than a stew, and it is much thinner than the goulash eaten in most restaurants outside Hungary. The so-called goulash as we know it, with its thick brown sauce, is called 'pörkölt' in Hungary. As is the case with so many traditional dishes, there are any number of varieties. The cattlemen naturally use beef, but mutton can also be used, or even pork. If it is prepared with pork and sauerkraut, it becomes the famous 'Székelygulyás.' The cook in one famous restaurant in Budapest also adds green beans, and during the grape harvest wine is sometimes added to the goulash served to grapepickers.
In the summer the visitor can go to small outdoor eating places called 'gulácarda', or goulash inns. Three different kinds of goulash are served, spooned piping hot out of pots and eaten with brown bread and caraway seeds.

Reisfleisch

Pork with rice

6 servings

- *3 tablespoons butter*
- *1 onion, finely chopped*
- *1 clove garlic, crushed*
- *2 pounds pork shoulder, cut into ½ inch cubes*
- *1 tablespoon paprika*
- *½ teaspoon salt*
- *Freshly ground black pepper*
- *5 cups beef broth*
- *1½ cups rice*
- *4 tablespoons heavy cream*
- *12 thin strips pimiento*

Heat the butter in a casserole and sauté the onions and garlic until softened. Add the pork and sauté until brown. Pour off the accumulated fat and add the paprika, salt, pepper and 2 cups broth. Cover and simmer 1 hour. Meanwhile, cook the rice in the remaining broth until all the liquid has been absorbed. Strain the pork and onions and reserve the cooking liquid. Combine the rice with the strained pork and onions and mold firmly into individual serving dishes. Stir the cream into the reserved cooking liquid and bring to a simmer. Pour a little of the sauce over each serving. Garnish with 2 strips of pimiento and serve immediately.

Székely gulyas

Pork goulash

6 servings

- *3 tablespoons butter*
- *4 onions, sliced*
- *1 teaspoon caraway seeds*
- *1 clove garlic, crushed*
- *1 tablespoon chopped fresh dill or 1 teaspoon dried dill weed*
- *½ teaspoon salt*
- *Freshly ground black pepper*
- *2½ pounds shoulder of pork, cut into 1 inch cubes*
- *½ cup water*
- *1 tablespoon paprika*
- *2 pounds sauerkraut*
- *½ cup sour cream*

Heat the butter in a casserole and sauté the onions until golden brown. Stir in the caraway seeds, garlic, dill, salt and pepper. Arrange the pork on top of the onion mixture and pour in the water. Cover and simmer gently 30 minutes. Check occasionally to see if the mixture is sticking to the pan and add water, 1 tablespoon at a time, if necessary. Add the paprika and sauerkraut and combine thoroughly. Cover and cook over very low heat 1 hour or until the pork is tender. Remove from the heat and stir in the sour cream. Serve from the casserole with boiled potatoes.

Kümmelfleisch

Caraway goulash

4 servings

- *2 pounds lean beef, cut into ¾ inch cubes*
- *1 onion, quartered*
- *½ teaspoon salt*
- *Freshly ground black pepper*
- *1 teaspoon crushed caraway seeds*
- *½ teaspoon paprika*
- *Pinch of ground cloves*
- *2 teaspoons vinegar*
- *Beef broth or water*

Place the beef, onion, salt, pepper, caraway seeds, paprika, cloves and vinegar in a heavy casserole. Add beef broth or water to just cover the ingredients, bring to a boil and skim the broth. Reduce the heat, cover and simmer 2 hours until beef is tender. Serve with boiled potatoes or buttered noodles.

Koloszvári gulyas

Goulash Klausenburg style

6 servings

- *2 tablespoons butter*
- *2 pounds beef chuck or round, cut into ¾ inch cubes*
- *2 onions, coarsely chopped*
- *1 clove garlic, crushed*
- *1 tablespoon paprika*
- *½ teaspoon caraway seeds*
- *¼ teaspoon marjoram*
- *1 teaspoon salt*
- *Freshly ground black pepper*
- *1½ cups beef broth or water*
- *4 medium sized potatoes, peeled and cubed*
- *2 green peppers, seeded and cut into strips*
- *4 tomatoes, peeled, seeded and sliced*
- *4 cups shredded white cabbage*

Heat the butter in a casserole. Add the beef and cook for 5 minutes until brown. Add the onions, garlic, paprika, caraway seeds, marjoram, salt, pepper and beef broth. Bring to a boil, reduce the heat and simmer, covered, for 1½ hours. Add the potatoes, peppers, tomatoes and cabbage and more water or broth if necessary. Cover and simmer for 25 minutes until the vegetables are tender.

Majoran tokany

Meat stew with sour cream

6 servings

- *6 tablespoons butter*
- *3 onions, chopped*
- *2 pounds rib steak or sirloin steak, cut into strips*
- *1 teaspoon salt*
- *Freshly ground black pepper*
- *½ teaspoon marjoram*
- *¾ cup white wine*
- *¾ cup water*
- *½ pound boiled ham, cut into strips*
- *1 cup sour cream*

Heat the butter in a large skillet. Add the onions and fry 4 to 5 minutes until golden. Add the beef and season with salt, pepper and marjoram. Sauté 3 to 4 minutes. Add the wine and water, bring to a boil and simmer, covered, for 1 hour. Add the ham and simmer for 30 minutes. Stir in the sour cream. Heat but do not boil. Serve with noodles.

Krautfleisch

Pork and cabbage stew

6 servings

- *2 pounds pork shoulder, cut into squares*
- *1 teaspoon salt*
- *Freshly ground black pepper*
- *6 tablespoons butter*
- *2 onions, chopped*
- *1 clove garlic, crushed*
- *1 tablespoon paprika*
- *½ tablespoon wine vinegar*
- *1 head white cabbage, shredded*
- *2 cups chicken broth*
- *6 tablespoons heavy cream, lightly beaten*
- *1 tablespoon chopped chives*

Season the pork with salt and pepper. Heat 3 tablespoons of the butter in a skillet and brown the pork on all sides. Remove from the pan. Heat the remaining butter and fry the onions with the garlic until golden. Add the paprika and wine vinegar and simmer for 1 minute, stirring constantly. Place the pork, onion mixture and cabbage in a casserole. Add the chicken broth and simmer gently for 1 hour. Transfer to a heated serving dish. Spoon the cream into the center of the dish and garnish with chives. Serve with boiled potatoes.

The Swiss city of Zurich enjoys a certain gastronomic fame, and one of its best known specialities is the 'Zürcher Geschnetzeltes', finely cut veal in a mushroom sauce.

The stewed pork and cabbage dish that you can find all over Central Europe is like many others of Hungarian origin. Pork and cabbage stew (recipe page 43, 4th column).

Zürcher Geschnetzeltes

Shredded veal Zürich style

6 servings

6 tablespoons butter
1 onion, finely chopped
1½ pounds veal, cut into very thin strips
1 teaspoon salt
Freshly ground black pepper
¾ cup dry white wine
½ pound button mushrooms
1 cup milk
½ cup half and half
1 tablespoon cornstarch dissolved in
2 tablespoons water

Heat 4 tablespoons butter in a skillet and sauté the onion until soft. Add the veal and sauté over high heat until onion and meat are golden brown. Add ½ teaspoon salt, pepper and wine and simmer, stirring frequently, for 15 minutes. In the meantime, heat the remaining butter in a saucepan and sauté the mushrooms 5 minutes. Season with the remaining salt and pepper. Stir in the milk and half and half and heat until simmering. Add the milk mixture to the veal and stir gently until the ingredients are thoroughly combined. Stir in the cornstarch mixture to thicken. Serve with potato pancake (recipe page 74).

Stiermarken is an Austrian province south of Vienna. It has contributed a great deal to the fame of Viennese cooking, *(recipe page 47, 1st column).*

Gefüllter Kalbsbraten

Stuffed veal

6 to 8 servings

- *1 leg of veal*
- *6 tablespoons butter*
- *3 large onions, chopped*
- *1 calf's kidney, chopped*
- *1 cup fresh breadcrumbs*
- *1 teaspoon salt*
- *Freshly ground black pepper*
- *2 egg yolks, beaten*

Cut the leg of veal lengthwise up up to the bone. Remove the bone and pound the meat flat. Heat 2 tablespoons butter in a frying pan. Add the onions and kidney and fry until lightly browned. Stir in the breadcrumbs, salt and pepper, remove from the heat and allow to cool slightly. Add the egg yolks to bind the mixture. Spread over the flattened inside of the leg of veal. Roll up and secure with string. Place in a roasting pan, add the remaining butter and cook in a preheated 350° oven, allowing 30 minutes per pound. Baste frequently. Serve with sour cream and a salad.

Thurgauer Leberspätzli

Shredded liver Thurgau style

4 servings

- *4 tablespoons butter*
- *2 onions, finely chopped*
- *½ pound calves' liver, ground*
- *2½ cups flour*
- *4 eggs*
- *⅓ cup water*
- *½ teaspoon salt*
- *Freshly ground black pepper*
- *¼ teaspoon marjoram*
- *¼ teaspoon sage*
- *2 tablespoons finely chopped parsley*

Heat 2 tablespoons of the butter in a skillet. Add half of the onions and cook for 4 minutes until softened. Place the fried onions and butter in a mixing bowl. Add the liver, flour, eggs, water, salt, pepper, marjoram, sage and parsley. Stir the mixture to combine the ingredients and then beat it steadily for 5 minutes, turning the mixture over and over to allow air to lighten it. Bubbles will appear in the mixture as it is beaten. Continue beating for another 6 or 7 minutes until the mixture is very light. Chill for 1 hour. Spread the mixture on the back of a cookie sheet. Dip a knife into hot water frequently and cut the mixture into matchstick-like strips. Drop the strips into simmering water and cook for 3 to 4 minutes. In the meantime, bring another large saucepan of salted water to boiling point. Drain the strips and cook in the second pan of water for 1 more minute. Drain and place on a hot serving plate. Heat the remaining butter and fry the remaining onion for 5 minutes until lightly browned. Pour the onion and hot butter over the liver (spatzli) and serve at once.

Pörkölt Borjumaj

Calves' liver paprika

4 servings

- *1 pound calves' liver*
- *2 tablespoons butter*
- *1 onion, chopped*
- *1 tablespoon paprika*
- *½ teaspoon salt*
- *Freshly ground black pepper*

Cut the liver into strips 2 inches long, ½ inch wide and ¼ inch thick. Heat the butter in a skillet, add the onion and fry over low heat for 5 minutes until softened. Sprinkle on the paprika and increase the heat. Add the liver and stir for 3 to 4 minutes until evenly browned. Season with salt and pepper and serve immediately.

Steirisches Wurzelfleisch

Pork stew from Stiermarken

6 servings

3 *tablespoons butter*
2½ *pounds shoulder of pork, cut into 1 inch pieces*
4 *onions, coarsely chopped*
1 *small turnip, cut into strips*
4 *carrots, cut into strips*
1 *bay leaf*
2 *whole cloves*
½ *teaspoon thyme*
½ *teaspoon salt*
Freshly ground black pepper
Beef broth or water
2 *pounds potatoes, peeled and diced*
Grated fresh horseradish

Heat the butter in a skillet and sauté the pork over high heat until nicely browned on all sides. With a slotted spoon, transfer the pork to a casserole. Add the onions, turnip, carrots, bay leaf, cloves, thyme, salt, pepper and enough broth or water to barely cover the ingredients. Bring to a boil, lower the heat and simmer, covered, 1 hour or until the pork is tender. Cook the potatoes in plenty of boiling salted water 15 to 20 minutes until tender. Serve the stew over the diced potatoes and garnish with a generous sprinkling of horseradish.

Appenzellerli

Pork Appenzell style

4 servings

16 *(1 ounce) slices pork tenderloin*
6 *tablespoons butter*
1 *onion, finely chopped*
1 *clove garlic, crushed*
½ *cup diced ham*
¼ *pound mushrooms, finely chopped*
½ *cup flour*
½ *cup dry white wine*
1 *tablespoon finely chopped parsley*
Pinch of rosemary
Pinch of sage
½ *teaspoon salt*
Freshly ground black pepper
1 *egg yolk*
⅔ *cup grated Appenzell cheese or substitute Gruyère or Swiss cheese*
2 *eggs, lightly beaten*
1 *cup fine dry breadcrumbs*

Pound the pork slices between 2 sheets of wax paper until very thin. Heat 2 tablespoons butter in a skillet and sauté the onion and garlic until soft. Add the ham and mushrooms and cook, stirring, 3 minutes. Add 1 tablespoon flour and cook 1 minute. Add the wine, parsley, rosemary, sage, salt and pepper and cook, stirring, until the mixture is thick. Remove from the heat and let cool. Add the egg yolk and cheese and combine thoroughly. Spread 8 of the pork slices with the mixture, top with the remaining pork slices and pinch the edges together to seal. Heat the remaining butter in a large skillet. Dredge each piece

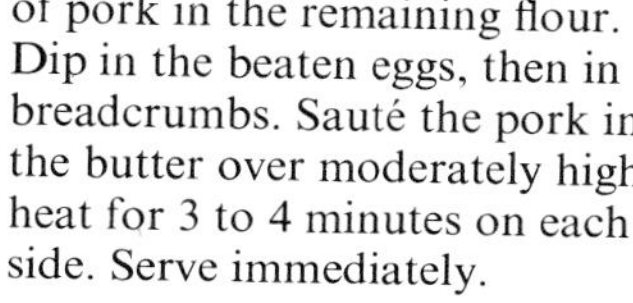

of pork in the remaining flour. Dip in the beaten eggs, then in breadcrumbs. Sauté the pork in the butter over moderately high heat for 3 to 4 minutes on each side. Serve immediately.

Pörkölt

Stewed pork

6 to 8 servings

6 *tablespoons butter*
4 *onions, chopped*
1 *tablespoon paprika*
3 *pounds pork shoulder, cut into small pieces*
1½ *teaspoons salt*
Freshly ground black pepper
1½ *cups chicken broth or water*
2 *green peppers, seeded and cut into strips*
6 *medium sized tomatoes, peeled and sliced*

Heat the butter in a skillet and fry the onions until golden. Sprinkle with paprika and add the pork. Season with salt and pepper. Brown the pork over high heat for 4 to 5 minutes. Add the chicken broth and bring to a simmer. Cover and cook over low heat 1 hour. Add the peppers and tomatoes and simmer for 15 minutes. Serve with macaroni.

Wiener Schnitzel

Fillet of veal Vienna style

4 servings

- *1 pound veal scallops*
- *⅓ cup flour seasoned with*
  - *½ teaspoon salt*
  - *Freshly ground black pepper*
- *1 egg, lightly beaten*
- *½ cup fine dry breadcrumbs*
- *4 tablespoons butter*
- *4 slices lemon*

Pound the veal scallops between 2 sheets of wax paper until very thin. Dredge each piece in seasoned flour. Dip in the egg, then in the breadcrumbs. Heat the butter in a large skillet and sauté the veal over moderately high heat until golden brown on both sides. Arrange the veal on a heated serving dish and garnish with lemon slices. Serve with parslied potatoes and a crisp green salad.

Emmentaler Schnitzel

Veal cutlets Emmenthal style

4 servings

- *4 (4 ounce) veal scallops*
- *Juice of 1 lemon*
- *½ teaspoon salt*
- *Freshly ground black pepper*
- *1 to 2 tablespoons grated Parmesan cheese*
- *1 egg*
- *½ cup fine dry breadcrumbs*
- *4 tablespoons butter*
- *4 thick slices Emmenthal (Swiss) cheese*

Pound the veal scallops between 2 sheets of wax paper until they are very thin. Sprinkle each side with lemon juice, salt, pepper and Parmesan cheese. Beat the egg lightly and stir in the breadcrumbs. Coat each scallop with some of the breadcrumb mixture. Heat the butter in a skillet and sauté the veal on 1 side for 2 to 3 minutes until golden brown. Turn the scallops and place a slice of cheese on each. Lower the heat, cover the pan and cook about 3 minutes more until the cheese is melted. Serve immediately with a crisp green salad.

Gespickte Kalbsvögerl

Larded veal birds

6 servings

- 2 *pounds veal, cut from the leg into 6 equal sized portions*
- 1 *teaspoon salt*
- *Freshly ground black pepper*
- 6 *slices bacon*
- 3 *tablespoons butter*
- 1 *onion, finely chopped*
- 1 *tablespoon tomato paste*
- 1 *cup chicken broth or water*
- 1 *tablespoon cornstarch*
- ½ *cup dry white wine*
- 1 *teaspoon lemon juice*

Season the veal with salt and pepper. Pound each piece until very thin and roll up tightly. Wrap a strip of bacon around each roll and secure with string. Heat the butter in a frying pan, add the onion and cook until soft and golden. Add the veal rolls and fry 5 to 10 minutes. Reduce heat and stir in tomato paste and chicken broth. Cover and simmer gently for 1 hour. Remove veal from pan, discard strings and keep warm. Combine cornstarch and wine and add to pan juices. Continue cooking for 3 to 5 minutes until sauce has thickened. Add lemon juice and pour sauce over veal rolls. Serve with rice and mushrooms.

Tafelspitz

Boiled beef

6 servings

- 6 *cups water*
- 2 *teaspoons salt*
- 2 *onions*
- 2 *carrots*
- 3 *sprigs parsley*
- 6 *peppercorns, crushed*
- 1 *bay leaf*
- 3 *pounds top or bottom round of beef*
- 3 *tablespoons chopped chives*
- 1½ *cups mayonnaise*

Place the water, salt, onions, carrots, parsley, peppercorns and bay leaf in a saucepan and bring to a boil. Add the beef, cover and simmer for 1½ to 2 hours. Remove the beef from the saucepan and cut into slices ½ inch thick. Arrange the beef on a heated serving dish and pour over 1 cup of the beef broth. Stir the chopped chives into the mayonnaise and serve separately as a sauce. Serve with boiled potatoes and applesauce.

Eszterházy rostélyos

Steak Esterházy

6 servings

- *2 pounds boneless chuck steak, in 1 piece*
- *1 teaspoon salt*
- *Freshly ground black pepper*
- *6 tablespoons butter*
- *2 turnips, peeled and cut into strips*
- *½ cup chopped parsley*
- *2 stalks celery, cut into thin slices*
- *2 onions, chopped*
- *4 tablespoons flour*
- *6 peppercorns, crushed*
- *1 tablespoon paprika*
- *2 cups beef broth*
- *2 cups sour cream*
- *1 tablespoon capers*
- *½ lemon, sliced*

Season the beef with salt and pepper. Heat the butter in a frying pan and brown the meat quickly on both sides over high heat. Remove from the pan and keep warm. In the same butter, fry the turnips, parsley, celery and onions for 5 minutes. Stir in the flour, peppercorns and paprika. Add the beef broth gradually, stirring constantly. Cover and simmer for 10 minutes. Arrange the meat in a casserole and pour over the sauce. Cover and simmer gently for 2 hours. Before serving, add the sour cream. Heat but do not boil. Slice the steak and garnish with capers and lemon slices.

Tocana

Transylvanian stew

6 to 8 servings

- *2½ pounds stewing veal*
- *1 teaspoon salt*
- *Freshly ground black pepper*
- *4 tablespoons butter*
- *8 small onions, sliced*
- *1½ cups chicken broth*

Cut the veal into 2 inch cubes and season with salt and pepper. Brown the veal for 15 minutes in the heated butter. Add the onions and chicken broth and bring to a boil. Reduce the heat and simmer, covered, for about 1¼ hours until most of the broth has been absorbed. Serve hot.

Znojemska pecene

Beef with gherkins

6 servings

- *2 pounds flank steak*
- *3 tablespoons butter*
- *½ cup sliced mushrooms*
- *1½ tablespoons chopped lean bacon*
- *1 teaspoon paprika*
- *½ teaspoon salt*
- *Freshly ground black pepper*
- *1 tablespoon chopped parsley*
- *2 dill pickles, coarsely chopped*
- *1 cup beef broth*

- *1 tablespoon butter, softened*
- *1 tablespoon flour*
- *½ cup sour cream*

Cut the beef in half lengthwise and pound each half until thin. Place one half on top of the other and trim to form a rectangle. Cut the trimmings into small pieces. Heat ½ the butter in a skillet. Add the beef trimmings, mushrooms and bacon and fry for 2 minutes. Remove from the heat and sprinkle with paprika. Season the beef with salt and pepper. Sandwich the beef trimmings, mushrooms, bacon, parsley and dill pickles between the slices of beef. Roll the meat like a jelly roll and tie with string. Heat the remaining butter in a large pan. Add the rolled beef and fry over high heat until browned. Remove beef from the pan. Discard the string and cut into thick slices. Combine 1 tablespoon butter with 1 tablespoon flour in a custard cup and add to the liquid in the pan. Add the remaining broth. Bring to a boil and simmer for 2 hours. Remove from the heat, stir in the sour cream and bring to simmering point. Pour a little sauce over the meat. Serve the remaining sauce in a sauceboat.

Gekochter Schweinschlegel

Boiled fresh ham

8 servings

- *1 fresh ham*
- *2 onions, sliced*
- *2 carrots, sliced*
- *1 parsnip, cubed*
- *1 small turnip, cubed*
- *1 clove garlic, crushed*
- *1½ teaspoons salt*
- *8 peppercorns, crushed*
- *¼ teaspoon allspice*
- *6 tomatoes, peeled and quartered*
- *½ teaspoon salt*
- *1½ cups dry white wine*

Place the ham in a pan. Add boiling water to cover and let stand for 3 minutes. Pour off the water. Add more water to cover, bring to a boil and skim off the scum that rises to the surface. Add the onions, carrots, parsnip, turnip, garlic and seasonings. Bring to a boil, reduce the heat and simmer gently for 3 to 3½ hours or until the ham is tender (30 minutes to the pound). Place the tomatoes in a pan. Sprinkle with salt and add the white wine. Bring to a boil, reduce the heat and simmer, stirring occasionally, until reduced to a thick sauce. Force through a strainer and keep warm. Pour the liquid off the ham when cooked and reserve for use in soups. Transfer the ham and vegetables to a serving dish, pour over the tomato sauce and serve.

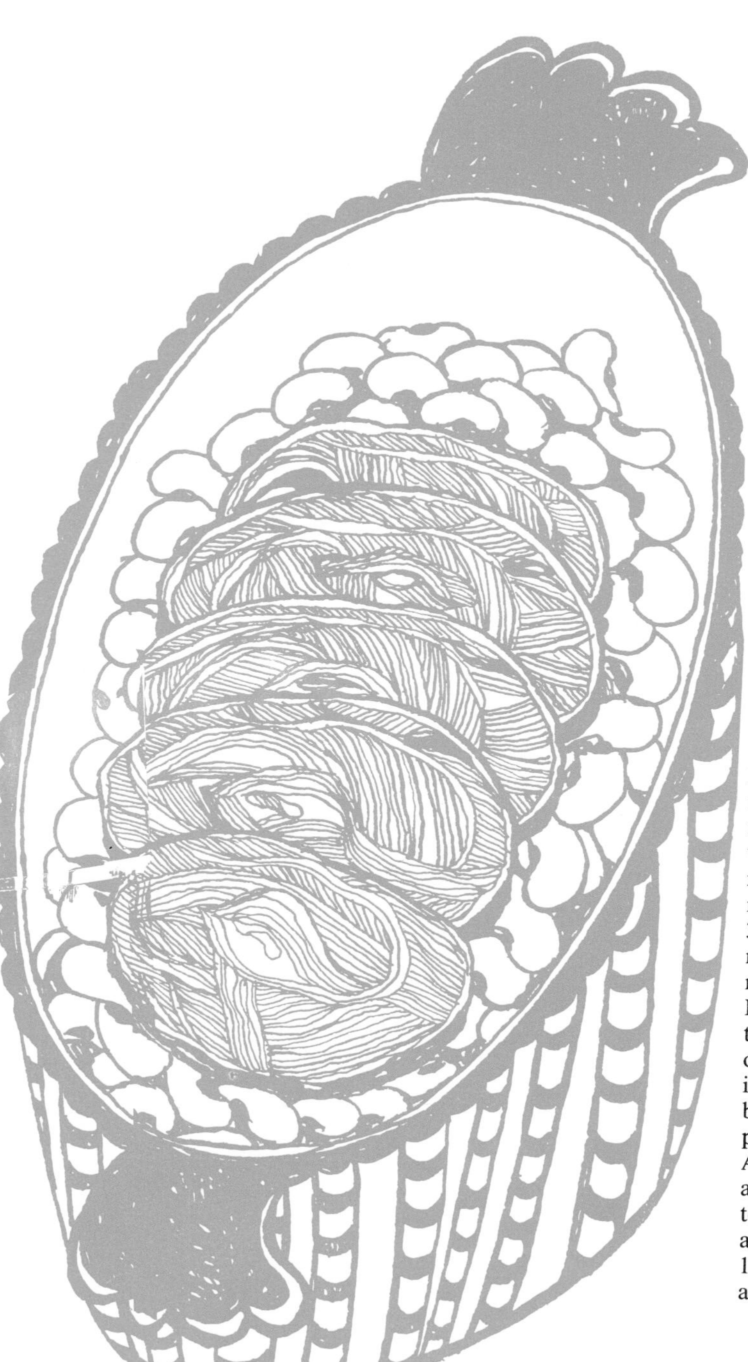

Bosnische schwarze Pfanne

Bosnian black pot

6 to 8 servings

- *4 pounds pork belly (fresh bacon), with rind*
- *2 tablespoons coarse salt*
- *1 to 2 cups water*
- *¼ pound bacon, diced*
- *1 onion, chopped*
- *1 cup beef broth*
- *2 green peppers, seeded and cut into strips*
- *2 (16 ounce) cans broad beans, drained*
- *½ teaspoon salt*
- *Freshly ground black pepper*
- *¼ teaspoon marjoram*
- *1 cup heavy cream*
- *2 tablespoons finely chopped parsley*

Make diamond shaped incisions in the pork rind and rub the rind with coarse salt. Pour water to a 1 inch depth into a roasting pan and add the pork, rind side down. Roast in a 325° oven 1 hour. Turn and roast 1 hour more until the rind is crisp and brown. Meanwhile, fry the bacon until the fat is rendered. Add the onion and fry until the bacon is crisp and the onion is golden brown. Add broth and green peppers and simmer 15 minutes. Add the beans, salt, pepper and marjoram and transfer to a casserole. Stir in the cream and parsley and simmer 10 to 15 minutes. Slice the meat and arrange on top of the beans.

Pork is delicious with sauerkraut, but in early summer, when the tender garden beans are ready, no one in Austria hesitates to substitute them for the more traditional accompaniment.

Bosnian black pot (recipe page 51, 4th column).

Schweinekotelett auf Sauerkraut

Pork chops with sauerkraut

4 servings

4 tablespoons butter
2 onions, chopped
1½ pounds sauerkraut
½ cup beef broth
½ cup red wine
1 green pepper, seeded and chopped
2 bay leaves
2 teaspoons paprika
⅛ teaspoon white pepper
4 pork chops
½ teaspoon salt
Freshly ground black pepper

Heat 2 tablespoons butter in a casserole and sauté the onions until golden brown. Add the sauerkraut and broth and simmer 30 minutes. Add the wine, green pepper, bay leaves, paprika and white pepper and simmer 30 minutes more. Meanwhile, heat the remaining butter in a skillet. Sprinkle the pork chops with salt and pepper and sauté over medium heat about 15 minutes on each side until golden brown and done. Arrange the chops on top of the sauerkraut in the casserole. Serve with broiled tomatoes, and corn on the cob or boiled potatoes.

Tender veal tongue is one of the pride and joys of Viennese cooking. Perhaps this has something to do with the white wine grown on the hills around Vienna that tastes so good with it.

Kalbszunge

Veal tongue

4 servings

- *1 (2 pound) veal tongue*
- *1 teaspoon salt*
- *1 carrot, sliced*
- *1 onion, quartered*
- *1 sprig parsley*
- *1 bay leaf*
- *1 clove*
- *4 peppercorns, crushed*
- *1 package frozen French cut green beans, cooked and chopped*
- *1 package frozen asparagus tips, cooked*
- *2 oranges, peeled and thinly sliced*
- *6 tablespoons cranberry jelly*

Soak the tongue in cold water 2 to 3 hours. Rinse thoroughly and sprinkle with salt. Place the tongue in a large casserole with the carrot, onion, parsley, bay leaf, clove and peppercorns and add water to cover. Bring to a boil, lower the heat and simmer, covered, 2½ hours until the tongue is tender. Drain the tongue, remove the skin and cut into ½ inch thick slices. Arrange the slices on a warm serving dish alternately with the green beans and asparagus tips. Surround with orange slices and top the orange slices with a spoonful of cranberry jelly. Serve with mashed potatoes.

Eingemachtes Kalbsfleisch

Veal ragout

4 servings

1½ pounds veal, cut into 1½ inch cubes
1 teaspoon salt
Freshly ground black pepper
3 tablespoons butter
1 onion, chopped
2 tablespoons flour
1½ cups chicken broth or water
1 cup mushrooms, sliced
4 tablespoons green peas
1 tablespoon chopped parsley
1 egg yolk
2 tablespoons milk
1 teaspoon lemon juice

Season the veal with salt and pepper. Heat the butter and brown the meat over high heat for 5 minutes. Remove the veal from the pan. Add the onion to the butter and fry until soft and golden. Stir in the flour and add the chicken broth gradually, stirring constantly until the sauce is thickened. Add the veal and mushrooms. Bring to a boil and simmer gently for 45 minutes. Add water if the sauce becomes too thick. Add the peas and parsley and cook for 10 minutes. Before serving, stir in the egg yolk combined with the milk and lemon juice. Heat thoroughly and serve.

Teleci gulas

Veal stew

4 servings

4 tablespoons butter
1¾ pounds stewing veal, cubed
1 teaspoon salt
Freshly ground black pepper
2 teaspoons caraway seeds, crushed
½ onion, chopped
1 carrot, diced
2 cups chicken broth
2 tablespoons flour
1 tablespoon chopped parsley

Heat the butter in a saucepan. Add the veal and fry until lightly browned on all sides. Season with salt, pepper and caraway seeds. Reduce the heat, cover and continue cooking for 7 to 8 minutes. Add the diced vegetables and fry for another 2 minutes, stirring occasionally. Add ½ of the broth, bring to a boil. Reduce the heat, cover and simmer for 1 hour or until the meat is tender. Remove the lid, increase the heat and allow almost all the broth to evaporate. Stir in the flour and add the parsley and remaining broth. Bring to a boil and simmer for another 10 minutes.

Pieds de porc

Pork hocks Geneva style

4 to 6 servings

3 tablespoons oil
6 fresh pork hocks
½ teaspoon salt
Freshly ground black pepper
2 carrots, chopped
2 large onions, chopped
2 cloves garlic, crushed
1 cup white wine
4 tomatoes, peeled, seeded, drained and chopped
White part of 1 leek, chopped
1 cup beef broth
¼ teaspoon dried rosemary
¼ teaspoon dried tarragon
1½ teaspoons mild (Dijon type) mustard
2 tablespoons fine dry breadcrumbs
1 tablespoon butter
½ pound mushrooms, chopped
1½ tablespoons cornstarch
¼ cup Madeira

Heat the oil in a large pan and fry the pork hocks 10 to 15 minutes until lightly browned. Season with salt and pepper, remove from the pan and keep warm. In the remaining oil, fry the carrots, onions and garlic until soft. Add the wine, tomatoes, leek, beef broth, rosemary and tarragon. Return the pork to the pan, cover and simmer for 3 hours. Remove the pork, drain and cut the meat from the bones. Reserve the cooking liquid. Place the meat in a buttered casserole, spread with mustard and sprinkle with breadcrumbs. Add the drained vegetables and bake in a preheated 400° oven for 20 minutes. (It will not dry out.) Heat 1 tablespoon butter in a frying pan and fry the mushrooms until lightly browned. Add 2 cups of the reserved cooking liquid. Dissolve the cornstarch in the Madeira and stir into the sauce. Simmer 2 minutes until thickened. Serve the sauce separately.

Rostélyos cigány módra

Roast beef Gypsy style

4 servings

- 2 *pounds rump steak, cut into 4 slices*
- ½ *teaspoon salt*
- *Freshly ground black pepper*
- 5 *tablespoons butter*
- 1 *onion, chopped*
- 3 *tablespoons flour*
- ½ *cup red wine*
- *Beef broth*
- 2 *tablespoons tomato purée*
- 1 *bay leaf*
- 1 *carrot, thinly sliced*
- 1 *leek, thinly sliced*
- 1 *green or red pepper, seeded and cut into thin strips*
- 8 *slices bacon, fried until crisp*

Pound the slices of beef between 2 sheets of wax paper. Sprinkle with salt and pepper and sauté quickly in 3 tablespoons butter until brown on both sides. Transfer to a casserole. In the same butter, sauté the onion until softened. Add the flour and cook 2 minutes. Add the wine and 1½ cups broth gradually, stirring constantly until the sauce is thickened. Add the tomato purée and bay leaf and pour over the beef in the casserole. Add more broth if necessary to barely cover the meat. Simmer, uncovered, 1½ hours, turning the meat occasionally. Add a little broth from time to time if the sauce becomes too thick. Meanwhile, heat the remaining butter in a saucepan and sauté the carrot, leek and pepper 2 minutes. Add broth to barely cover the vegetables and simmer 10 minutes. Place the slices of beef on individual serving plates and top with the vegetables. Garnish each serving with 2 strips of bacon.

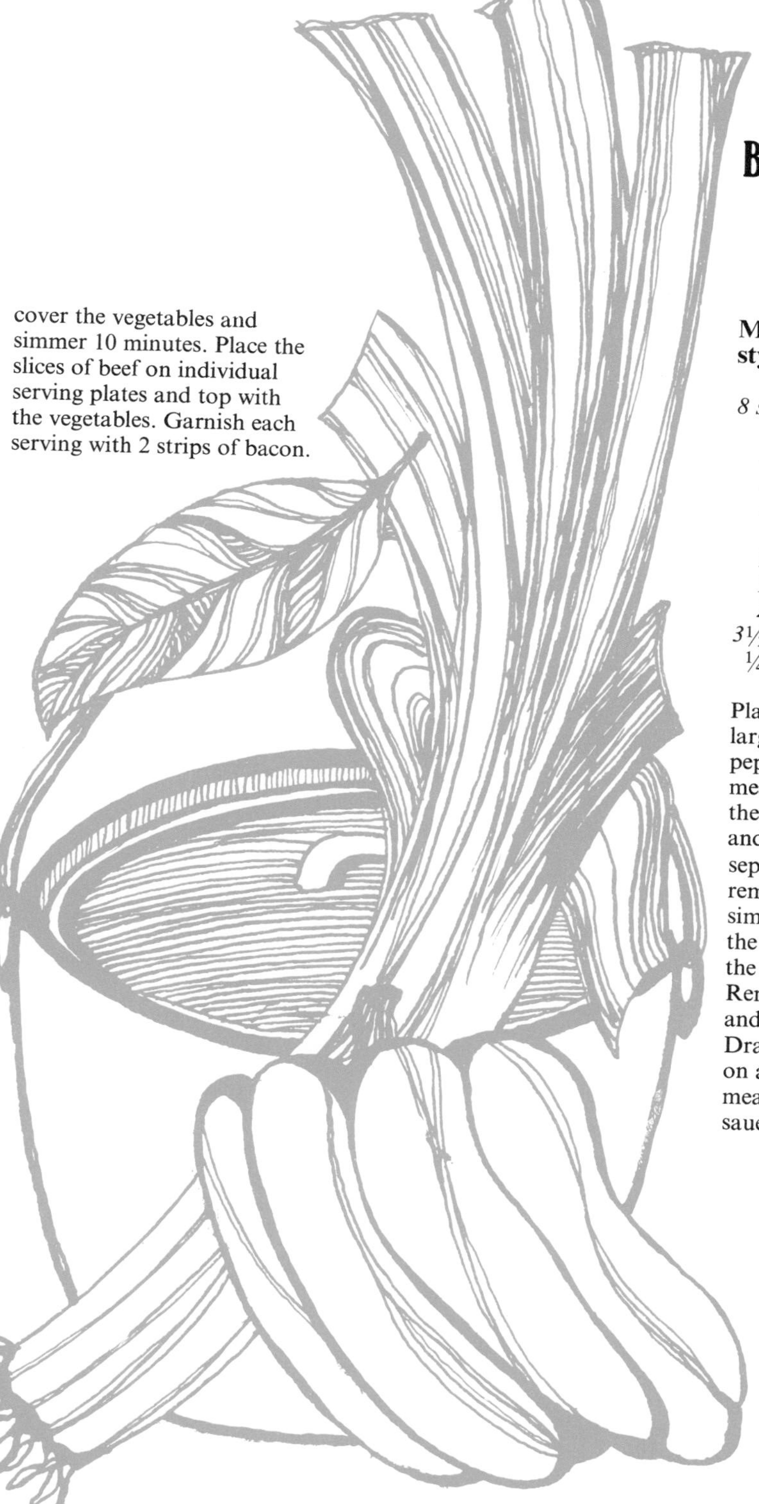

Berner Platte

Meat and sauerkraut Bern style

8 servings

- 1 *veal tongue*
- 1 *pound stewing beef*
- 1 *teaspoon salt*
- *Freshly ground black pepper*
- 1 *pound lean salt pork*
- 1 *pound spare ribs*
- 2 *smoked sausages*
- 3½ *pounds sauerkraut*
- ¼ *cup water*

Place the tongue and beef in a large pan and add the salt, pepper and water to cover the meat. Bring to a boil and skim the broth. Lower the heat, cover and simmer 2½ to 3 hours. In a separate pan, combine the remaining ingredients and simmer, covered, 1 hour. Drain the tongue and beef and remove the skin from the tongue. Remove the salt pork, spareribs and sausage from the sauerkraut. Drain the sauerkraut and place on a warm platter. Slice the meats, arrange on top of the sauerkraut and serve.

Hammelkeule

Roast leg of lamb

6 to 8 servings

1 (5 to 6 pound) leg of lamb, bone in
1 teaspoon salt
Freshly ground black pepper
½ teaspoon powdered thyme
2 cloves garlic, slivered
2 tablespoons olive oil
2 onions, quartered
6 tablespoons plum brandy or Kirsch
½ cup beef broth
½ cup red wine
1 tablespoon cornstarch dissolved in 2 tablespoons cold water

Rub the lamb with a mixture of salt, pepper and powdered thyme. Cut slits in the meat and insert slivers of garlic. Rub with olive oil, and place on a rack in a roasting pan. Add the onions. Roast the lamb, uncovered, in a preheated 450° oven for 15 to 20 minutes. Reduce the heat to 350° and continue roasting 20 minutes to the pound or until a meat thermometer registers 175°. Baste occasionally while cooking. Pour the Kirsch over the lamb. Remove lamb from the rack and keep it warm. Add the beef broth and red wine to the pan juices. Stir in the cornstarch paste to form a medium thick sauce. Serve with green beans and potatoes sprinkled with cumin.

Potée Fribourgeoise

Stew from Fribourg

6 servings

2½ to 3 pounds boneless beef shoulder or chuck, cut into 2 inch cubes
3 cups beef broth
1 onion, sliced
1 whole clove
1 bay leaf
1 teaspoon salt
Freshly ground black pepper
1 small head white cabbage, cut into wedges
3 carrots, coarsely chopped
1 leek, coarsely chopped
1 parsnip, coarsely chopped
3 medium sized potatoes, peeled and thickly sliced

Place the beef, broth, onion, clove, bay leaf, salt and pepper in a casserole. Bring to a boil, lower the heat and simmer, covered, 1½ hours. Add the cabbage, carrots, leek and parsnip and cook 30 minutes. Add the potatoes and cook another 30 minutes until the potatoes are tender. Serve with dill pickles, salted cucumbers or other sweet/sour condiments.

Schnitz und Drunder

Bacon and apple stew

4 servings

- ¾ *pound dried apple slices*
- 2 *tablespoons sugar*
- 1 *teaspoon water*
- 1 *pound lean smoked bacon, sliced*
- 1½ *cups beef broth*
- 3 *medium sized potatoes, peeled and thickly sliced*

Soak the apples in lukewarm water to cover for 2 hours. Place the sugar and water in a casserole and stir over moderately high heat until the sugar caramelizes. Drain the apples and add to the casserole with the bacon and broth. Bring to a boil, reduce the heat and simmer, covered, 1 hour. Add the potatoes and cook 30 minutes until the potatoes are tender. Serve from the casserole.

Zürcher Ratsherrntopf

Counselor's stew Zurich

4 servings

- 1 *pound potatoes, peeled*
- 7 *tablespoons oil*
- 4 *tablespoons butter*
- 1 *pound fresh peas, shelled*
- ½ *pound carrots, peeled and chopped*
- 3 *tablespoons finely chopped shallots or scallions*
- ½ *pound mushrooms, sliced*
- 4 *slices bacon*
- ¼ *pound calves' liver, diced*
- 1 *sweetbread, diced*
- 1 *kidney, diced*
- ½ *pound sirloin steak, diced*
- 1 *teaspoon salt*
- *Freshly ground black pepper*

Form the potatoes into balls with a melon ball scoop. Cook 5 minutes in plenty of boiling salted water and drain. Heat 4 tablespoons oil in a skillet. Dry the potato balls thoroughly and sauté in the oil over low to medium heat 10 to 15 minutes until nicely browned on all sides. Meanwhile, prepare the remaining ingredients. Heat 2 tablespoons butter in a saucepan. Add the peas and carrots, cover and cook over the lowest possible heat about 15 minutes or until tender. Heat the remaining butter in a skillet and sauté the shallots and mushrooms about 5 minutes. Remove from the pan and keep warm. Fry the bacon until crisp and drain on paper towels. Heat the remaining oil in a skillet and sauté the liver, sweetbread, kidney and sirloin steak about 5 minutes until golden brown. Remove from the heat and season with ½ teaspoon salt and pepper. To serve, arrange the cooked vegetables attractively on a heated platter and sprinkle with the remaining salt and pepper. Spoon the meat mixture over the vegetables and serve.

Chifteluta

Meat patties

4 servings

- *4 slices day old bread, crusts removed*
- *2 tablespoons milk*
- *1 pound ground beef*
- *1 teaspoon salt*
- *Freshly ground black pepper*
- *2 cloves garlic, crushed*
- *1 tablespoon chopped parsley*
- *¼ teaspoon paprika*
- *3 tablespoons oil*

Crumble the slices of bread and soak them in the milk for 10 minutes. Squeeze out excess milk. Add all the remaining ingredients except the oil and stir together lightly. Divide the mixture into 4 portions and shape each portion into a hamburger patty. Heat the oil in a skillet and fry the patties 5 minutes on each side until brown and crisp on the outside.

Neuenburger Leberpastetchen

Liver patties Neuenburg

6 servings

- *2 tablespoons butter*
- *1 onion, chopped*
- *½ pound calves' liver, chopped*
- *½ teaspoon salt*
- *Freshly ground black pepper*
- *1 egg*
- *1 egg yolk*
- *2 tablespoons fine dry breadcrumbs*
- *½ teaspoon marjoram*
- *½ teaspoon sage*
- *1 tablespoon parsley*
- *1 package frozen individual patty shells, baked*
- *1 egg, beaten*

Heat the butter in a frying pan, add the onion and fry gently until soft. Remove from the heat and mix thoroughly with the liver, salt, pepper, egg, egg yolk, breadcrumbs and herbs. Remove the center lids from the thawed patty shells and fill the shells with the liver mixture. Place on a buttered baking sheet. Replace the lids loosely, brush the patty shells with beaten egg and bake in a preheated 400° oven for 25 minutes until golden brown.

Mititei

Barbecued sausages

4 servings

- *1 pound beef, ground twice*
- *1 teaspoon salt*
- *Freshly ground black pepper*
- *¾ teaspoon powdered dried thyme*
- *¾ teaspoon powdered dried marjoram*
- *¼ teaspoon powdered bay leaf*
- *1 onion, minced*
- *1 small clove garlic, minced*
- *3 tablespoons cold water*
- *2 tablespoons oil*

Combine the beef with all the remaining ingredients, except the oil. Cover and set aside for 6 hours. Shape into thin sausages 1 inch in diameter and 2 inches long. Brush with oil and grill over charcoal or under the broiler for 8 minutes on each side until crisp and brown.

Töltött káposzta

Stuffed cabbage with sauerkraut

4 servings

- *1 pound ground pork*
- *¾ cup half cooked rice*
- *⅓ cup diced boiled ham*
- *2 eggs, lightly beaten*
- *1 onion, finely chopped*
- *½ clove garlic, crushed*
- *1 teaspoon salt*
- *Freshly ground black pepper*
- *8 large whole cabbage leaves*
- *2 tablespoons butter*
- *1½ pounds sauerkraut, flaked with a fork*
- *½ pound bacon, sliced*
- *1½ cups water*
- *1 cup sour cream*

Combine the ground pork, rice, ham, eggs, onion, garlic, salt and pepper and mix thoroughly. Simmer the cabbage leaves in salted water for 4 minutes. Drain and cool. Place a portion of the meat mixture on each cabbage leaf and roll into a neat package by tucking in the sides and securing with a thread. Butter a deep casserole. Add ½ the sauerkraut and top with the stuffed leaves. Arrange the bacon on top and cover with the remaining sauerkraut. Add the water, cover, bring to a boil and simmer gently for 1½ hours. Spoon on the sour cream, heat thoroughly and serve hot.

Churer Fleischtorte

Meat pie from Chur

4 servings

- *1 package frozen patty shells, formed into 1 round of dough*
- *2 tablespoons butter*
- *1 onion, chopped*
- *2 slices bacon, chopped*
- *½ pound ground beef*
- *½ pound ground pork*
- *1 tablespoon flour*
- *¼ cup red wine*
- *¼ cup beef broth*
- *½ teaspoon salt*
- *¼ teaspoon marjoram*
- *½ teaspoon paprika*
- *1 egg, beaten*

Roll out ⅔ of the dough into a 9 inch pie plate. Heat 2 tablespoons butter in a skillet. Add the onion and bacon and fry over low heat for 3 minutes. Add the ground meats and fry until lightly browned. Stir the flour into the wine and beef broth until smooth. Add the salt, marjoram and paprika and combine with the meats. Simmer for 5 minutes. Let cool slightly and spread over dough. Roll out remaining pastry to form a lid. Brush the edges with beaten egg and place the lid over the base. Press the edges to seal. Prick with a fork in several places. Bake in a preheated 375° oven for 40 to 45 minutes until golden brown.

Chicken stewed in a pot together with vegetables can be found almost everywhere in the world, but in Rumania they vary it by adding white beans.

Pui Românese

Chicken stew

4 servings

- *1 (3 to 3½ pound) chicken, cut into serving pieces*
- *1 teaspoon salt*
- *Freshly ground black pepper*
- *3 tablespoons butter*
- *2 carrots, finely chopped*
- *2 kohlrabi or turnips, finely chopped*
- *1 tablespoon finely chopped parsley*
- *1 tablespoon sugar*
- *2 cups chicken broth*
- *1 cup fresh peas*
- *2 tablespoons flour combined with*
- *1 tablespoon softened butter*

Sprinkle the chicken pieces with salt and pepper. Heat the butter in a casserole and sauté the chicken a few pieces at a time over medium heat until golden brown on all sides. Remove from the casserole and keep warm. Add the carrots, kohlrabi, parsley and sugar and cook slowly, stirring until the sugar caramelizes. Return the chicken to the pan and add 1 cup broth. Bring to a boil, lower the heat and simmer, covered, 30 minutes until chicken is tender. Add the peas and cook 10 minutes more. Add the remaining broth, bring to a simmer and add the flour/butter mixture a little at a time, stirring constantly. Simmer 3 more minutes to thicken the sauce. Serve from the casserole.

Sacher Huhn

Sacher chicken

6 servings

- *1 (3½ to 4 pound) roasting chicken*
- *½ pound bulk sausage*
- *1 pair sweetbreads, blanched, peeled and chopped*
- *¾ teaspoon salt*
- *Freshly ground black pepper*
- *2 tablespoons butter*
- *3 tablespoons Madeira*

Remove the giblets from the cavity of the chicken. Chop the liver and reserve the remaining parts for another use. In a bowl, combine the chopped liver, sausage, sweetbreads, ¼ teaspoon salt and pepper. Heat the butter in a skillet and sauté the mixture about 7 minutes, stirring occasionally. Pour off the accumulated fat. Add the Madeira and simmer 2 minutes. Sprinkle the cavity of the chicken with the remaining salt and pepper and stuff with the sausage mixture. Truss the chicken securely and place on a rack in a roasting pan. Roast 10 minutes in a 400° oven. Reduce the heat to 350° and roast 1 hour more until the juices run clear when pricked with a fork. Place the chicken on a platter, remove the trussing strings and serve.

Eingemachtes Huhn

Chicken stew

4 servings

- *1 (3 pound) chicken, cut into 4 pieces*
- *1 teaspoon salt*
- *Freshly ground black pepper*
- *¼ teaspoon marjoram*
- *½ teaspoon paprika*
- *4 tablespoons butter*
- *2 tablespoons olive oil*
- *2 onions, cut into rings*
- *2 carrots, sliced*
- *1 leek, cut into rings*
- *1 pound canned lima beans, drained*
- *½ cup chicken broth*
- *1 teaspoon lemon juice*

Rub the chicken pieces with salt, pepper, marjoram and paprika. Heat 2 tablespoons butter and 2 tablespoons olive oil in a skillet and brown the chicken pieces on all sides for 10 minutes. Heat the remaining butter in a casserole, add the onions and fry until golden. Add carrots, leek and lima beans and cook for 15 minutes. Add chicken pieces and broth and simmer for 50 to 60 minutes until the chicken is tender. Add lemon juice before serving. Serve with a cabbage salad and sliced green peppers.

Csirke tejfolben

Chicken in sour cream

4 servings

3 pounds chicken breasts
½ cup flour
3 tablespoons butter
1 teaspoon salt
Freshly ground black pepper
Bouquet garni
1 cup chicken broth
2 teaspoons paprika
1 cup sour cream

Bouquet garni:
3 or 4 sprigs parsley
½ bay leaf
2 sprigs thyme
½ small onion
2 cloves
½ stalk celery

Tie the bouquet garni ingredients in a small piece of cheesecloth that can be removed from the broth.

Dredge the chicken pieces in flour. Heat the butter in a large skillet and fry the chicken until golden brown on both sides. Season with salt and pepper. Add the bouquet garni, chicken broth and paprika. Bring to a boil and simmer for 25 minutes. Discard the bouquet garni. Stir in the sour cream and heat without boiling.

Csirke bácska

Chicken Bacska style

4 to 6 servings

3 slices bacon, cut into small pieces
2 onions, finely chopped
1 tablespoon paprika
2 (2 pound) chickens, cut into serving pieces
½ teaspoon salt
1 cup chicken broth
2 tablespoons butter
1 cup raw rice
2 green peppers, seeded and cut into strips
4 medium sized tomatoes, peeled, seeded and sliced
1 cup water
1 tablespoon chopped parsley

Fry the bacon in a heavy skillet until the fat is rendered. Add the onions and fry 4 to 5 minutes, until the onions are golden and the bacon is crisp. Add the paprika. Sprinkle the chicken with salt and place in the skillet. Add the chicken broth and bring to a boil. Simmer for 25 minutes. Heat the butter in a saucepan, add the rice and stir for 2 to 3 minutes. Add the rice, peppers, tomatoes and 1 cup water to the chicken. Cover and cook in a preheated 375° oven for 20 to 25 minutes until the rice is tender and has absorbed the liquid. Garnish with chopped parsley.

Hühnerragout

Chicken ragout

6 servings

1 (3½ to 4 pound) chicken
1¼ teaspoons salt
Freshly ground black pepper
3 tablespoons butter
⅓ cup finely chopped celery
2 carrots, peeled and finely chopped
1 parsnip, finely chopped
1 cup button mushrooms
2 cups chicken broth
1 tablespoon lemon juice
1 tablespoon flour combined with ½ tablespoon softened butter
2 tablespoons finely chopped parsley

Sprinkle the chicken inside and out with 1 teaspoon salt and pepper. Heat the butter in a casserole and sauté the chicken over high heat until nicely browned on all sides. Reduce the heat to the lowest possible point, cover the casserole and place an asbestos pad under it. Cook 20 minutes, turning the chicken once. Remove the chicken from the pan and set aside until it is cool enough to handle. Discard the skin and bones and cut the meat into bite sized pieces. Place in a clean casserole and add the celery, carrots, parsnip, mushrooms, ½ the broth, lemon juice, remaining salt and pepper. Bring to a boil, reduce the heat and simmer, partially covered, for 30 minutes. Stir in the remaining broth, the flour mixture and parsley and simmer 20 minutes more.

Paprikás csirke

Paprika chicken

4 servings

2 tablespoons olive oil
2 onions, finely chopped
1 clove garlic, crushed
1 tablespoon paprika
½ teaspoon cumin
1 (2½ to 3 pound) chicken, cut into serving pieces
½ teaspoon salt
2 cups chicken broth
2 carrots, peeled and sliced
2 tablespoons tomato paste

Heat the oil in a casserole and sauté the onions and garlic until golden brown. Stir in the paprika and cumin and cook 1 minute. Arrange the chicken pieces on top of the onions and sprinkle with salt. Pour in the broth and add the carrots. Bring to a simmer, cover and cook over low heat 25 minutes. Stir the tomato paste into the broth and simmer, covered, 25 minutes more until chicken is tender. Serve with macaroni or other pasta.

The fine flavor of 'edelsüsz' paprika gives the Hungarian paprika chicken its distinctly piquant taste, (recipe page 63, 4th columm).

Pollo alla montanara

Chicken in wine sauce

4 servings

- 2 *(2 pound) frying chickens, cut into serving pieces*
- 1 *teaspoon salt*
- *Freshly ground black pepper*
- 4 *tablespoons flour*
- 3 *tablespoons olive oil*
- ⅓ *cup shredded boiled ham*
- 1¼ *cups dry white wine*
- ½ *teaspoon sage*

Season the chicken pieces with salt and pepper and dredge with flour. Heat the oil in a large skillet. Add the chicken and fry until golden brown on all sides. Add the ham and sauté for another 2 minutes. Add the wine, and sage. Cover and bake in a preheated 375° oven for 40 minutes or until tender.

Chicken in wine sauce.

As Viennese as the Viennese Waltz in the 'Wiener Backhendl', a deep-fried young chicken which is always eaten in the wine cellars outside Vienna, where you can taste the 'Heurige', a young wine from the last vintage.

Fried chicken (recipe page 66, 1st column).

Backhendl

Fried chicken

4 servings

- 2 *(2 pound) chickens, cut into serving pieces*
- ½ *cup flour, seasoned with 1 teaspoon salt Freshly ground black pepper*
- 3 *eggs, lightly beaten*
- 1 *cup fine dry breadcrumbs*
- 1 *cup butter*
- 1 *cup shortening*
- 8 *sprigs parsley*

Dry the chicken pieces thoroughly. Dredge them in flour, then dip in the beaten eggs and coat with breadcrumbs. Heat the butter and shortening together until sizzling and fry the chicken pieces a few at a time until golden brown and crisp. Drain on paper towels and place in a shallow ovenproof casserole. Bake in a 400° oven 15 minutes. Fry the parsley sprigs in the butter and shortening for a few minutes until crisp. Garnish the chicken with the fried parsley and serve.

Gebratenes Entchen

Roast duckling

3 to 4 servings

- 1 *tablespoon butter*
- 1 *cup button mushrooms*
- 1 *cup white breadcrumbs*
- 6 *tablespoons cream*
- 2 *teaspoons chopped parsley*
- 1 *small onion, chopped*
- ⅛ *teaspoon marjoram*
- ½ *teaspoon salt Freshly ground black pepper*
- 2 *eggs, lightly beaten*
- 1 *(3 to 4 pound) duckling*

Heat the butter, add the mushrooms and fry gently for 5 minutes. Soak the breadcrumbs in the cream and stir in the mushrooms, parsley, onion, marjoram, salt, pepper and eggs. Rub the inside of the duck with salt and pepper and stuff with the prepared mixture. Prick the duck skin all over with a fork. Place duck on a rack in a roasting pan in a preheated 450° oven for 10 minutes. Reduce the heat to 350° and continue roasting for 1¼ hours.

Kachnas cervenym-zelim

Duck and red cabbage

4 servings

- 1 *small red cabbage, thinly shredded*
- 2 *teaspoons salt*
- 3 *tablespoons bacon fat*
- 1 *bay leaf Freshly ground black pepper*
- 1 *(4 pound) duck*
- 1 *tart apple, peeled, cored and chopped*
- 1 *small orange, peeled and sliced*
- ½ *cup chopped lean ham*

Place the cabbage in a bowl, toss with 1 teaspoon salt and set aside 2 hours. Squeeze the cabbage dry. Heat the bacon fat in a saucepan and add the cabbage, bay leaf and pepper. Cover and cook over low heat 30 to 40 minutes, stirring occasionally. Stuff the cavity of the duck with the apple, orange and ham. Truss the duck, sprinkle the skin with the remaining salt and pepper and prick all over with a fork. Place on a rack in a roasting pan and roast in a 350° oven 1¼ to 1½ hours until tender. Prick the skin occasionally during the roasting period. Place the duck on a heated platter and remove all the trussing strings. Reheat the cabbage and spoon it around the duck.

Kacsa Kukoricaval

Duck with sweet corn

4 servings

- 2 *slices day old white bread*
- 3 *tablespoons milk*
- 1 *(16 ounce) can sweet corn, drained*
- ½ *teaspoon salt Freshly ground black pepper Liver of the duck*
- 3 *thin slices lean bacon*
- 1 *(4 to 5 pound) duck*
- 1 *teaspoon coarse salt*

Crumble the bread and soak in the milk. Squeeze out the excess milk. Add the corn, salt and pepper. Chop the duck liver and bacon and mix with the corn. Stuff the duck with this mixture and secure the opening with toothpicks. Prick the duck skin with a fork and rub with coarse salt. Place on a rack in a roasting pan and roast in a preheated 450° oven for 10 minutes. Reduce heat to 350° and continue cooking for 1½ hours or until tender.

Kaninchenpastete

Rabbit pie

6 servings

Short crust pastry:

- 2½ *cups sifted all purpose flour*
- ¼ *teaspoon salt*
- 6 *tablespoons butter*
- 6 *tablespoons shortening*
- 6 *to 8 tablespoons cold water*

Filling:

- 1 *(3 to 3½ pound) rabbit or chicken, cut into 4 pieces*
- 1 *teaspoon salt*
- ½ *cup minced bacon*
- 1 *cup minced lean pork*
- *Freshly ground black pepper*
- *Pinch of marjoram*
- ½ *bay leaf, crumbled*
- 1 *tablespoon chopped parsley*
- 2 *eggs, lightly beaten*
- 1 *egg yolk, lightly beaten*

To prepare the pastry, sift the flour and salt into a bowl. Cut the butter and shortening into the flour with a pastry blender or 2 knives until the mixture resembles coarse meal. Add the water, using only enough to make the dough stick together, and gather the dough into a ball. Wrap in wax paper and refrigerate 1 hour. Meanwhile, place the rabbit in a pan and add water to cover. Bring to a boil and skim the broth. Add ½ teaspoon salt, lower the heat and simmer, covered, about 40 minutes until the meat is tender. Drain and let stand until cool enough to handle. Fry the bacon in a skillet until the fat is rendered. Add the pork and continue cooking until the bacon is crisp and the pork nicely browned. Remove from the heat, drain off the accumulated fat and let cool. Remove the skin from the rabbit, chop the meat into small cubes and add to the bacon and pork. Add the remaining salt, pepper, marjoram, bay leaf, parsley and eggs and combine thoroughly. Roll out ½ the pastry and fit into a deep 8 inch pie tin. Add the filling. Roll out the remaining pastry and place over the filling, pinching the edges together to seal. Prick the pastry with a fork and brush with beaten egg yolk. Bake in a 350° oven 40 minutes or until the crust is golden brown. Remove from the oven and let cool.

Coniglio arrosto alla ticinese

Rabbit Ticino style

4 servings

- 1 *young rabbit, cut into serving pieces*
- 1 *teaspoon salt*
- *Freshly ground black pepper*
- 1 *teaspoon dried thyme*
- 1 *teaspoon dried marjoram*
- 1 *teaspoon dried rosemary*
- 3 *juniper berries, crushed*
- ⅓ *cup diced boiled ham*
- 3 *tablespoons olive oil*
- ½ *cup dry white wine, heated*
- ½ *cup hot water*
- ½ *cup Marsala wine*

Season the rabbit with salt, pepper, thyme, marjoram, rosemary and juniper berries. Place in a casserole with the ham and add the olive oil. Cook uncovered in a preheated 400° oven for 25 minutes until brown. Add the wine and water and continue cooking for another 45 minutes, basting occasionally. Add the Marsala wine and continue cooking 20 minutes or until the meat is tender. Serve with mashed potatoes.

Gebratene Gans

Roast goose

8 servings

- 1 *young (9 pound) goose*
- 2 *teaspoons salt*
- *Freshly ground black pepper*
- 2 *teaspoons marjoram*
- 4 *sweet apples, peeled, cored and sliced*
- 8 *sugar cubes*
- *Red currant jelly*

Rub the goose skin and cavity with salt and pepper. Sprinkle the marjoram inside the cavity. Stuff the goose with the apples and sugar cubes. Prick the goose skin all over with a fork. Place on a rack. Pour 1 cup of water into the roasting pan. Roast goose uncovered in a preheated 450° oven for 15 minutes. Baste the goose and reduce the heat to 350°. Continue cooking for 3 hours, basting occasionally and adding more water to the pan if necessary. Remove from the oven, carve and serve with red currant jelly.

Vegetable dishes

The art of stuffing paprikas was brought to Hungary three hundred years ago by the Turks. The Hungarians in turn exported this art to Austria.

Gefüllte Paprikaschoten

Stuffed peppers

4 servings

- *4 green or red peppers*
- *2 hard boiled eggs, finely chopped*
- *¼ pound ham, cut into thin strips*
- *1 egg*
- *2 medium sized potatoes, cooked and mashed*
- *3 tablespoons grated Parmesan cheese*
- *4 tablespoons olive oil*
- *½ teaspoon salt*
- *Freshly ground black pepper*
- *1 onion, finely chopped*
- *1 tablespoon flour*
- *1 tablespoon paprika*
- *½ cup water*
- *2 tablespoons wine vinegar*
- *2 tablespoons tomato paste*
- *1 teaspoon sugar*

Cut the tops off the peppers and reserve. Remove the seeds and membranes from the peppers. In a bowl, combine the hard boiled eggs, ham, raw egg, potatoes, cheese, 2 tablespoons oil, ¼ teaspoon salt and pepper. Stuff the peppers with the mixture and replace the tops. Heat the remaining oil in a casserole and sauté the onion until golden brown. Add the flour and paprika and cook, stirring, 2 minutes. Add the water gradually, stirring constantly until a thick sauce forms. Stir in the vinegar, tomato paste, sugar, remaining salt and pepper and simmer 10 minutes. Arrange the stuffed peppers in the casserole. Cover and cook over very low heat 30 minutes.

Reis mit Bohnen

Rice with green beans

4 to 6 servings

- *3 tablespoons oil*
- *1 onion, finely chopped*
- *1 clove garlic, crushed*
- *2 tablespoons tomato paste*
- *2 cups beef broth*
- *1 cup rice*
- *½ pound tender young green beans, trimmed and cut into 1 inch lengths*
- *¼ teaspoon salt*
- *Freshly ground black pepper*
- *¼ teaspoon marjoram*
- *2 tablespoons grated Parmesan cheese*

Heat the oil in a heavy casserole and sauté the onion and garlic until softened. Stir in the tomato paste and beef broth and bring to a boil. Add the rice and stir once with a fork. Reduce the heat to the lowest possible point, cover the pan and cook 10 minutes. Stir in the beans, salt, pepper and marjoram. Cover and continue cooking 25 to 30 minutes until the liquid has been absorbed by the rice and the beans are tender. Stir in the cheese and serve.

Gefüllte Zwiebeln

Stuffed onions

8 servings

- *8 uniformly sized onions*
- *2 slices white bread, crusts removed*
- *½ cup hot milk*
- *2 tablespoons butter*
- *⅓ cup ground beef*
- *⅓ cup chopped cooked ham*
- *2 eggs*
- *1 tablespoon finely chopped parsley*
- *½ teaspoon salt*
- *Freshly ground black pepper*
- *2 tablespoons fine dry breadcrumbs*
- *¼ cup grated Parmesan cheese*
- *1 cup beef broth, simmering*

Peel off the outer skin of the onions but do not slice off the ends. Bring plenty of salted water to a boil and add the onions. Lower the heat, cover and simmer 10 minutes. Drain immediately and let the onions stand in cold water until cool. Meanwhile, soak the bread in the hot milk. Heat 1 tablespoon butter in a small skillet and sauté the ground beef until it has lost all trace of pink. Pour off all the accumulated fat and place the beef in a bowl. Squeeze the milk out of the bread slices, crumble and add to the beef. Add the ham, eggs, parsley, salt and pepper and combine thoroughly. Cut the tops off the onions and carefully scoop out the insides, leaving a ¼ inch shell. Slice off the bottoms. Chop the scooped out pulp finely and combine with meat mixture. Stuff the onions and arrange them in a buttered shallow baking dish. Sprinkle with breadcrumbs and cheese and dot with the remaining butter. Pour the simmering broth into the pan and bake the onions in a 350° oven 30 minutes. Serve immediately.

Sarmalutsa

Stuffed sauerkraut

6 to 8 servings

- *12 large whole green cabbage leaves*
- *2 pounds sauerkraut*
- *1 pound ground pork*
- *¾ pound ground beef*
- *1 cup raw rice*
- *3 cloves garlic, crushed*
- *1 teaspoon salt*
- *Freshly ground black pepper*
- *4 tablespoons butter*
- *1½ large onions, chopped*
- *2 teaspoons paprika*
- *2½ cups beef broth*
- *6 tablespoons sour cream*

Simmer the cabbage leaves in boiling water for 5 minutes until softened. Drain and rinse under cold running water. Place ½ the sauerkraut in a large pan, cover with the cabbage leaves and top with the remaining sauerkraut. Leave for 36 hours. Combine the pork, beef, rice, garlic, salt and pepper with 4 to 6 tablespoons of warm water to form a smooth mixture. Remove the cabbage leaves from the sauerkraut, divide the meat mixture into 12 portions and place on the leaves. Roll each leaf, tucking in the sides and tie with a thread or secure with a toothpick. Heat the butter and fry the onions for 3 minutes. Add the paprika and fry for another 3 minutes. Add the drained sauerkraut, stir to mix and top with the stuffed leaves. Season with salt and pepper. Add 1½ cups beef broth and bring to a boil. Cover and simmer for 45 minutes. Add ¾ cup beef broth and continue simmering for 1 hour. Mix remaining beef broth with the sour cream and add to the sauerkraut. Remove from the heat and serve immediately.

Karfiol Wiener Art

Viennese cauliflower

4 to 6 servings

- 1 *pound sweetbreads*
- 5 *anchovies*
- 1 *medium sized whole cauliflower*
- 2½ *tablespoons butter*
- ½ *teaspoon salt*
- *Freshly ground black pepper*
- 1 *tablespoon flour*
- 4 *tablespoons milk*
- 2 *egg yolks, lightly beaten*
- 4 *tablespoons cream*
- 1½ *tablespoons finely chopped parsley*
- 2 *tablespoons grated Parmesan cheese*
- 3 *tablespoons breadcrumbs*

Cover the sweetbreads with boiling water and allow them to stand for 5 minutes. Rinse under cold water, drain, peel and cut into small cubes. Rinse the anchovies to remove excess salt. Drain and chop the anchovies. Cook the cauliflower in boiling, salted water for 15 minutes until tender. Drain and keep warm. Heat 1½ tablespoons butter in a skillet, add the sweetbreads and fry gently for 4 minutes. Season with salt and pepper and remove from heat. Heat 1 tablespoon butter in a saucepan and stir in the flour until blended. Add the milk gradually, stirring to form a thick sauce. Remove sauce from heat and add the beaten egg yolks and cream. Return to the heat for 3 minutes, stirring constantly. Do not allow the sauce to boil. Add sweetbreads and anchovies. Place the cauliflower in a buttered casserole and cover with the sauce. Combine the parsley, Parmesan cheese and breadcrumbs and sprinkle over the cauliflower. Dot with butter and bake in a preheated 400° oven for 10 minutes or until lightly browned. Serve hot.

Papet Vaudois

Leek dish from Vaud

4 servings

- 4 *large potatoes, peeled and sliced*
- 4 *large leeks, cut into rings*
- 1 *cup beef broth*
- 1 *tablespoon flour*
- 2 *tablespoons milk*
- 1 *teaspoon salt*
- *Freshly ground black pepper*
- ¼ *teaspoon dried basil*
- ¼ *teaspoon dried thyme*
- ⅛ *teaspoon ground nutmeg*
- ½ *pound bacon, cut into slices*
- ½ *pound bratwurst sausage, in one piece*

Place layers of potatoes and leeks in a casserole. Add the beef broth, cover and simmer over a low heat 40 to 45 minutes. Stir together the flour and milk and add to the casserole. Season with salt, pepper, basil, thyme and nutmeg. Simmer the bacon and sausage in boiling water for 10 minutes. Cover the leek dish with slices of bacon and place the sausage on top. Cover and simmer gently over low heat for 10 minutes. Slice the sausage and arrange in the center of the dish for serving.

Spinat Pizokel

Spinach dumplings

- 2½ *cups flour*
- 1½ *teaspoons salt*
- *Freshly ground black pepper*
- 1 *cup milk*
- 1 *cup water*
- 6 *eggs*
- ½ *cup butter*
- 2½ *cups fine dry breadcrumbs*
- 1 *tablespoon finely chopped parsley*
- 1 *tablespoon finely chopped chives*
- 2 *packages frozen chopped spinach, cooked*
- ½ *cup grated Parmesan cheese*

Place the flour, salt and pepper in a bowl. Add the milk and water and beat until smooth. Add the eggs, 1 at a time, beating well after each addition. Heat ½ the butter in a skillet and sauté the breadcrumbs, stirring constantly until golden brown. Add the breadcrumbs, parsley and chives to the batter. Drain the spinach in a colander, pressing out as much liquid as possible. Add the spinach to the batter. Cover and set aside at least 1 hour. Bring plenty of salted water to a simmer. Form small dumplings using a tablespoon and slip them into the simmering water a few at a time. Remove them with a slotted spoon when they rise to the surface and keep warm while the remaining dumplings are cooking. Arrange on a heated serving dish and sprinkle with cheese. Serve a tomato sauce separately.

Paprika Tomaten Gemüse

Peppers and tomatoes

4 servings

- ½ *pound bacon, diced*
- 2 *onions, cut into rings*
- 1 *clove garlic, crushed*
- 4 *green and/or red peppers, seeded and cut into strips*
- 1 *pound tomatoes, peeled, seeded and cut into wedges*
- ¼ *teaspoon salt*
- *Freshly ground black pepper*
- ¼ *teaspoon thyme*
- ½ *cup dry white wine*
- 1 *cup diced soft cheese, such as Port Salut*

Fry the bacon in a casserole until the fat is rendered. Pour off all but 2 tablespoons of the accumulated fat. Add the onions and garlic and cook 5 minutes. Add the peppers and tomatoes and cook over low heat 20 minutes, stirring occasionally. Add salt, pepper, thyme and wine and simmer 5 minutes more. Add the cheese and remove from the heat when the cheese is just melted. Serve from the casserole with dark bread.

This cabbage strudel is not a sweet. It is, in fact, a full-flavored winter dish.

Krautstrudel

Cabbage stuffed strudel

4 to 6 servings

Dough:
- 2 *cups flour*
- ½ *teaspoon salt*
- 1 *egg*
- 1 *tablespoon butter, melted*
- 6 *to 8 tablespoons water*

Filling:
- ¼ *pound bacon, diced*
- 1 *onion, finely chopped*
- 1 *teaspoon paprika*
- 1 *small white cabbage, shredded*
- ½ *cup sour cream*
- ½ *teaspoon salt*
- *Freshly ground black pepper*
- ¼ *cup finely chopped red pepper*
- 4 *tablespoons melted butter*

Sift the flour and salt onto a board and make a well in the center. Combine the egg, butter and 6 tablespoons water and pour into the well. Begin kneading from the center outward and continue until the dough is smooth. Do not add additional water unless it is needed to make the dough stick together. Roll the dough out as thinly as possible into a rectangle. Place on a floured tea towel and brush with additional melted butter. Cover and let rest 30 minutes. To prepare the filling, fry the bacon in a skillet until the fat has rendered. Add the onion and continue frying until the bacon is crisp and the onion brown. Add the paprika and cook 1 minute. Stir in the cabbage and cook over low heat 10 minutes, stirring occasionally to prevent burning. Remove from the heat, add sour cream, salt and pepper and let cool completely. Spread the cabbage mixture on the dough and sprinkle the red pepper on top. Roll up with the aid of the tea towel and place on an oiled baking sheet. Brush with butter and prick with a fork. Bake in a 375° oven 30 minutes, basting with butter occasionally.

Though this cake is made from carrots it is in fact a delicious dessert and may be served plain or with whipped cream.

Burgunya paprikás

Potato paprika

4 servings

- 3 *slices bacon, diced*
- 2 *onions, chopped*
- 1 *tablespoon paprika*
- 4 *large potatoes, peeled and diced*
- 2 *green peppers, seeded and thinly sliced*
- 4 *tomatoes, peeled, seeded and sliced*
- ¾ *pound smoked sausage, sliced*
- *Water*

Fry the bacon in a casserole until the fat has rendered. Add the onions and sauté until golden brown. Stir in the paprika and cook, stirring constantly for 2 minutes. Add the potatoes, 1½ green peppers, tomatoes, sausage and water to barely cover the ingredients. Bring to a boil, lower the heat and simmer 20 minutes, stirring occasionally. Taste for seasoning, garnish with the remaining peppers and serve.

Rösti

Potato pancake

6 servings

- 2 *pounds potatoes*
- 4 *slices bacon, finely chopped*
- 1 *onion, finely chopped*
- 4 *tablespoons butter*
- ½ *teaspoon salt*
- *Freshly ground black pepper*

Peel the potatoes and grate them coarsely. Using two 8 to 9 inch skillets with sloping sides, fry the bacon until the fat has rendered. Add ½ the onion to each skillet and fry until the bacon is crisp and the onion lightly browned. Add 2 tablespoons butter to each skillet and, when it is melted, add the potatoes, pressing down on them with the back of a spatula. Sprinkle with half the salt and pepper and cook over medium heat 15 minutes, pressing the potatoes occasionally with the spatula. Invert each pancake onto a plate and slide back into the skillets. Sprinkle with the remaining salt and pepper and cook 15 minutes more. Serve directly from the skillet or cut into triangles and serve with Shredded veal Zurich style or Shredded liver Thurgau style (recipes page 46).

Schaffhauser Bölletünne

Onion pie from Schaffhausen

4 to 6 servings

- ½ *recipe short crust pastry (page 67)*
- 3 *tablespoons butter*
- 1½ *pounds onions, thinly sliced*
- 1 *tablespoon flour*
- 4 *eggs*
- 1½ *cups heavy cream*
- ½ *teaspoon salt*
- ¼ *teaspoon caraway seeds, crumbled*

Roll out the pastry on a floured board and line a 9 inch tart tin or pie plate with the pastry. Heat the butter in a skillet and sauté the onions until softened. Place the flour, eggs, cream, salt and caraway seeds in a mixing bowl and beat with a wire whisk until thoroughly combined. Stir in the onions with a wooden spoon. Pour the filling into the pastry shell and bake the pie in a 350° oven 40 minutes until the top is nicely browned. Cut into wedges and serve immediately.

Aargauer Rüeblitorte

Carrot cake from Aargau

6 servings

- 5 *eggs, separated*
- ¾ *cup sugar*
- *Juice and rind of 1 lemon*
- 1 *teaspoon cinnamon*
- ¼ *teaspoon cloves*
- 1½ *cups ground almonds*
- 1½ *cups coarsely grated carrots*
- ½ *teaspoon salt*
- 2 *tablespoons cornstarch*
- 1 *teaspoon baking powder*
- 8 *tablespoons fine dry breadcrumbs*
- 1 *tablespoon butter, melted*
- 2 *tablespoons powdered sugar*

Beat the egg yolks, sugar, lemon juice and rind until thick and creamy. Stir in the cinnamon, cloves, ground almonds and carrots. Mix together the salt, cornstarch, baking powder and 6 tablespoons breadcrumbs and add the butter. Beat the egg whites until stiff and gently fold into the mixture. Butter a 9 inch spring form cake pan, coat with the remaining breadcrumbs and pour the batter into the cake pan. Bake in a preheated 350° oven for 50 minutes. Dust with powdered sugar and allow to cool completely. Refrigerate overnight before serving.

Repasaláta

Red beet salad

4 servings

- 3 *tablespoons red wine vinegar*
- 1 *tablespoon sugar*
- ½ *teaspoon salt*
- ½ *teaspoon caraway seeds*
- 1 *tablespoon horseradish*
- 1 *pound cooked red beets, peeled and sliced*
- 4 *tablespoons mayonnaise*
- 1 *tablespoon capers*
- 2 *tablespoons chopped gherkins*
- 1 *hard boiled egg, chopped*
- 2 *tablespoons finely chopped parsley*

Combine the vinegar, sugar, salt, caraway seeds and horseradish. Pour over the beets and refrigerate at least 3 hours. Drain the beets, cut the slices into strips and place in a salad bowl. Combine the mayonnaise, capers, gherkins and egg and toss the beets with the dressing. Sprinkle with parsley and serve.

Mamaliga

Baked corn

4 servings

- 3½ *cups water*
- 1 *teaspoon salt*
- 1 *cup corn meal*
- 2 *tablespoons butter*
- ½ *cup sour cream*
- 6 *to 8 slices Greek feta cheese or Rumanian brynza cheese (optional)*
- 4 *eggs, poached or hard boiled*

Bring the water to a boil, add the salt and gradually stir in the cornmeal and butter. Cook for 15 minutes until all the water has been absorbed and the mixture is thick. Spread the mixture in a small buttered baking dish and top with the sour cream. Place in a preheated 450° oven for 7 to 8 minutes or until golden. Remove from the oven and serve hot with slices of cheese and poached or hard boiled eggs.

Spárgasaláta

Mushroom and asparagus salad

4 servings

- 6 *tablespoons oil*
- ½ *pound mushrooms, quartered*
- ½ *pound asparagus tips, cooked or canned*
- 4 *medium sized tomatoes, peeled, seeded and cut into wedges*
- 1 *green pepper, seeded and cut into strips*
- 4 *gherkins, sliced*
- 1 *lettuce head, shredded*
- 2 *tablespoons vinegar*
- 1 *teaspoon salt*
- *Freshly ground black pepper*

Heat the oil in a skillet and fry the mushrooms over low heat for 10 minutes. Remove from the heat and cool. Combine the mushrooms with the asparagus tips, tomatoes, green pepper and gherkins. Toss lightly with the lettuce. Season with vinegar, salt and pepper and pour over any oil left from cooking the mushrooms.

Salate de vinete

Eggplant salad

6 servings

- 2 *(1 pound) eggplants*
- 6 *tablespoons oil*
- 2 *tablespoons vinegar*
- 1 *teaspoon salt*
- *Freshly ground black pepper*
- 3 *cloves garlic, crushed*

Place the eggplants in a preheated 350° oven and roast uncovered for 1 hour until the skin is wrinkled. Remove eggplants from the oven and allow to cool slightly. Cut in half lengthwise and scoop out the pulp. Mash the pulp until smooth. Add the oil and vinegar gradually, beating constantly until well blended. Stir in the salt, pepper and garlic and chill in the refrigerator for 2 hours before serving.

Desserts and cakes

In Austria plums are the fruit usually used for dumplings, but when the apricots that grow along the shores of the Donau are ripe, they are used as well.

Pflaumenknödel

Plum dumplings

20 dumplings

- 2¼ *cups sifted flour*
- ½ *teaspoon salt*
- 4 *tablespoons butter*
- 2 *eggs, lightly beaten*
- ⅓ *to ½ cup milk*
- 20 *fresh plums, seeded*
- 20 *sugar cubes*
- 2 *tablespoons butter*
- 1 *cup fine dry breadcrumbs*
- 2 *tablespoons sugar*
- *Powdered sugar*

Sift the flour and salt together into a bowl. Cut the butter into the flour with a pastry blender or 2 knives. Add the eggs and just enough milk to make a stiff dough. Roll the dough out on a floured board and cut into 20 squares large enough to enclose the plums. Place a sugar cube in the cavity of each plum and wrap in a square of dough. Pinch the edges of the dough together with wet fingertips to seal the dough. Cook the dumplings, a few at a time, in simmering salted water for 10 minutes. Remove with a slotted spoon and drain. Heat the butter in a skillet and brown the breadcrumbs and the sugar, stirring constantly. Roll the dumplings in the breadcrumbs and dredge in powdered sugar. Serve immediately.

Schneenockerl

Snow balls

6 servings

- 4 *egg whites*
- ½ *cup sugar*

- 2 *cups milk*
- 1 *cup water*
- 6 *tablespoons sugar*
- 2 *tablespoons flour*
- 2 *egg yolks, beaten*
- 1 *teaspoon vanilla*

Beat the egg whites until soft peaks form. Add the ½ cup sugar gradually and continue beating until very stiff. Combine the milk, water and 6 tablespoons sugar in a large shallow pan and bring to a simmer, stirring occasionally. With 2 spoons, form "snow balls" out of the egg white mixture. Add to the barely simmering milk and poach 1 to 2 minutes. Turn the "snow balls" and cook another minute. Remove them with a slotted spoon and drain on paper towels. Add ¼ cup of the hot milk to the flour and stir until the mixture is smooth. Stir in ¼ cup more milk and add the mixture to the egg yolks, beating constantly. Add the egg yolk mixture to the remaining milk and cook, stirring constantly until the custard thickens. Remove from the heat and stir in the vanilla. Let the custard cool and spoon into individual dishes. Float the "snow balls" on top of the custard and serve.

Snowballs are the favorite dessert of all Austrian children.

The half-moon shaped sandwiches that are always served at the Viennese 5 o'clock coffee hour call to mind the time when the Turks besieged Vienna in the seventeenth century.

Crescent rolls, (recipe page 78, 1st column).

Kipfeln

Crescent rolls

20 rolls

- ½ *cup milk*
- 1 *package dry yeast*
- 1 *tablespoon sugar*
- ¼ *cup butter, melted and cooled*
- 1¾ *to 2 cups flour*
- *Pinch of salt*
- 1 *egg white combined with 2 teaspoons milk*

Heat the milk to lukewarm. Sprinkle in the yeast and stir to dissolve. Stir in the sugar and the butter. Sift the flour with the salt into a bowl. Add the flour to the milk mixture gradually. Turn the dough out onto a floured board and knead until very smooth and elastic. Place the dough in an oiled bowl, cover with a damp cloth and let rise 1 hour until doubled in bulk. Turn the dough out onto the board and knead for a few minutes. Roll it out as thinly as possible and cut into 5 inch triangles. Starting at the base of a triangle, roll each piece up and bend the ends into a crescent shape. Moisten the point of the triangles so they do not unroll. Place the rolls on an oiled baking sheet, cover and let rise 45 minutes until they double in bulk. Brush with the egg white mixture and bake in a 350° oven for 30 minutes or until lightly browned.

Marillenknödel

Apricot dumplings

16 servings

- 2 *pounds unpeeled boiled potatoes*
- 4 *tablespoons flour*
- 2 *tablespoons heavy cream*
- 1½ *tablespoons butter, melted*
- 1 *egg*
- ½ *teaspoon salt*
- 16 *dried apricots, soaked in water*
- 16 *sugar cubes*
- 4 *tablespoons butter*
- ¾ *cup fine dry breadcrumbs*
- 2 *tablespoons sugar*

Peel the potatoes and force through a ricer. Beat in the flour, cream, butter, egg and salt and mix to a smooth dough. Refrigerate for 1 hour. Drain the apricots and place a sugar cube in the center where the pit was removed. Roll out the dough. Divide it into 16 pieces and wrap an apricot in dough to form a ball. Drop the dumplings in boiling salted water a few at a time, and boil briskly for 10 minutes. Remove with a slotted spoon and transfer to a heated serving dish. Heat the butter in a heavy skillet, add the breadcrumbs and cook until golden brown. Add the sugar, mix well and sprinkle over the dumplings before serving.

Honigleckerli

Honey cookies

Makes 48 2 inch cookies

- 1 *cup (4 ounces) ground filberts*
- 1 *cup (4 ounces) ground almonds*
- 1 *cup sugar*
- 2 *tablespoons honey*
- 3 *egg whites*
- ½ *cup flour*
- *Grated rind of 1 orange*
- 8 *tablespoons powdered sugar*
- 2 *teaspoons lemon juice*

Combine the filberts, almonds, sugar, honey, 2 egg whites, flour and grated orange rind and knead until a smooth dough is formed. Refrigerate for 1 hour. Dust a board with powdered sugar to prevent sticking and roll the dough into a rectangle ¼ inch thick. Cut into squares or shapes. Butter a baking sheet and dust with flour. Place the cookies on the baking sheet and bake in a preheated 300° oven for 20 to 25 minutes until lightly browned. Remove cookies immediately and cool on a wire rack. Combine the powdered sugar, remaining egg white and lemon juice. Brush the cookies with this glaze while still warm. Honey cookies taste even better if they are left to mature for 2 or 3 days.

Topfenkipfeln

Cream cheese crescents

20 to 24 rolls

- 1 *recipe kipfeln dough (page 79)*
- ½ *cup butter*
- ½ *cup cream cheese*
- 1 *cup flour*
- 1 *egg*
- 2 *tablespoons water*

Prepare the kipfeln dough as directed on page 79. Beat the butter until creamy. Add the cream cheese and beat until light and fluffy. Add the flour gradually and beat until smooth. Add half the cream cheese mixture to the kipfeln dough and knead on a floured board until smooth and elastic. Place in an oiled bowl, cover and let rise until doubled in bulk. Turn the dough out onto the board and knead for a few minutes. Roll it out as thinly as possible and cut into 5 inch triangles. Roll pieces of the remaining cream cheese mixture between your hands, forming 3 inch long ropes. Place 1 at the base of each triangle and roll up as directed in the recipe for kipfeln. Place on an oiled baking sheet, cover and let rise 45 minutes until doubled in bulk. Combine the egg and water and brush the rolls with the mixture. Bake in a 400° oven 15 to 20 minutes or until golden brown.

Buchteln

Nut crescents

Makes 4 dozen

Dough:

1 *package dry yeast*
¼ *cup lukewarm water*
¼ *cup sugar*
¼ *cup milk*
½ *cup butter*
4 *cups flour*
¼ *teaspoon salt*
3 *whole eggs*
5 *egg yolks, lightly beaten*
½ *teaspoon vanilla*

Filling:

½ *cup ground filberts*
½ *cup ground walnuts*
2 *tablespoons fine dry breadcrumbs*
1 *tablespoon butter, melted*
½ *cup cream*
½ *cup sugar*
½ *teaspoon vanilla*

2 *tablespoons butter, melted*

Sprinkle the yeast over the lukewarm water. Add the sugar and stir to dissolve. Leave in a warm place for 5 to 10 minutes. Heat the milk, reduce heat and add the butter. Stir until the butter dissolves. Allow the milk to cool, then combine with the yeast mixture. Sift the flour and salt into a large bowl. Make a well in the center and pour in the yeast and milk mixture, eggs, egg yolks and vanilla. Work the flour into the other ingredients to form a smooth dough. Shape into a ball and place in a lightly buttered bowl. Cover and let stand in a warm place for 1 hour or until doubled in bulk.

To prepare the filling, combine the nuts, breadcrumbs, butter, cream, sugar and vanilla to form a paste. Refrigerate until needed. Punch the dough down and knead for 5 minutes. Roll into a rectangle ¼ inch thick. Cut into 3 inch squares and spread with the nut filling. Roll each square jelly-roll fashion and form into crescent shapes. Place on a buttered cookie sheet and brush with melted butter. Cover with a cloth and allow to rise for ½ hour. Bake in a preheated 350° oven for 15 to 20 minutes until golden brown. Nut crescents may also be filled with fruit, other nut mixtures or preserves.

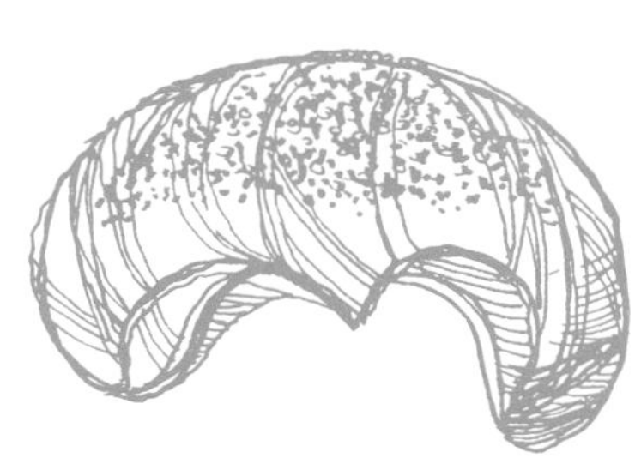

Nusskipfeln

Almond crescents

Dough:

1 *package dry yeast*
6 *tablespoons lukewarm milk*
2 *egg yolks*
2 *cups flour*
6 *tablespoons sugar*
¼ *teaspoon salt*

Filling:

¾ *cup sugar*
½ *cup water*
1 *tablespoon butter*
3 *(4 ounce) packages slivered blanched almonds, finely ground*
1 *tablespoon dark rum*
1 *teaspoon vanilla*

Glaze:

1 *egg, lightly beaten*

Sprinkle the yeast over the the lukewarm milk and stir to dissolve. Beat the egg yolks into the yeast mixture. Sift together the flour, sugar and salt and add to the yeast mixture gradually. Turn the dough out onto a well floured board and knead until smooth and elastic. Place the dough in an oiled bowl, cover and let rise in a warm place 1 hour or until doubled in bulk. Meanwhile, prepare the filling. Combine the sugar and water in a saucepan and heat, stirring until the sugar dissolves. Remove from the heat and stir in the butter until melted. Add the almonds, rum and vanilla and combine thoroughly. The mixture will be pasty. Punch the dough down and roll it out on a floured board to an ⅛ inch thickness. Cut into 3 × 4 inch rectangles. Spread a little of the filling down the center of a a rectangle lengthwise. Fold in half and pinch the edges together to seal. Bend into half moon shapes and place on a buttered baking sheet. Cover and let rise 30 minutes. Brush the crescents with the beaten egg and bake in a 375° oven 20 minutes. Cool on a wire rack.

The strudel casing around the apple must be crisp and paper-thin. Besides apples, other fruit used to make strudel include plums and apricots.

Apfelstrudel

Apple strudel

8 servings

- ½ *recipe strudel dough (page 73)*
- 3 *large apples*
- ½ *cup raisins*
- ½ *cup chopped walnuts*
- *Grated rind of ½ lemon*
- ¾ *cup sugar*
- ¼ *cup melted butter*
- ¼ *cup powdered sugar*

Prepare the strudel dough and roll it out as directed on page 73. Peel, core and cut the apples into thin slices. Place them in a bowl with the raisins, walnuts, lemon rind and sugar and toss gently. Spread the apple mixture on the dough and drizzle half the butter over it. Roll up the strudel with the aid of the tea towel and place, seam side down, on a buttered baking sheet. Prick the dough with a fork and brush with the remaining butter. Bake in a 350° oven 45 minutes. Let the strudel cool. Sift on the powdered sugar and serve.

In both Austria and Hungary, pastry-making reaches its perfection. The ordinary housewife can bake pies and cakes that are the envy of pastry chefs anywhere else in the world. The most difficult pastry of all is a really good strudel, with its almost endless number of paper-thin, flaky, golden pastry layers surrounding fillings of apple, cottage cheese or a soft mixture of poppyseed and nuts. It is impossible to decide whether the best strudel comes from Austria or from Hungary (where it is called 'rétes'.) The only real way to make good strudel dough is to spend years learning the art. The dough must first be kneaded into an elastic ball, and then thrown firmly onto the table from a height of at least three feet, until the dough becomes almost rubbery. Then the table should be covered with a clean sheet, sprinkled with flour. The ball is then rolled out into a thin sheet and this sheet is gently pulled by hand (with extreme care taken so that it does not tear) until, according to tradition, it is thin enough to read a newspaper through it.

The turban form of the Viennese 'Gugelhopf' recalls the influence of the Turks, who only just failed to take the city in the seventeenth century.

Gugelhupf

Marmor cake

10 servings

- ½ *cup butter*
- ¾ *cup sugar*
- 4 *eggs*
- 2½ *cups flour*
- ¼ *teaspoon salt*
- 2½ *teaspoons baking powder*
- *Grated rind of 1 lemon*
- 6 *tablespoons light cream*
- 3 *squares (3 ounces) semisweet chocolate, grated*
- ¼ *cup ground almonds*
- ½ *cup powdered sugar*

Beat together the butter and sugar until light and creamy. Beat in the eggs, 1 at a time. Fold in the flour, salt and baking powder. Divide the batter into 2 bowls. Add the grated lemon rind and 3 tablespoons cream to one bowl. Add the grated chocolate and remaining cream to the second half. Butter a fluted ring pan (kugelhupf pan) and sprinkle evenly with ground almonds, pressing them gently into the flutes. Fill the pan with ⅓ of the lemon mixture, add all of the chocolate mixture and finally the remaining lemon batter. Bake in a preheated 350° oven for 40 to 45 minutes. Unmold, coat with powdered sugar while still warm and allow to cool.

Kaiserschmarren

Emperor's pancake

4 servings

- ½ *cup flour*
- 5 *tablespoons sugar*
- ½ *teaspoon salt*
- 1 *cup milk*
- 5 *eggs, separated*
- 2 *tablespoons butter*
- *Powdered sugar*

Sift the flour, sugar and salt together into a bowl. Add the milk gradually, beating constantly. Add the egg yolks 1 at a time and beat until well blended. Beat the egg whites until stiff and stir ⅓ into the batter. Carefully fold in the remainder. Over moderately high heat, melt 1 tablespoon butter in an 8 to 9 inch skillet with sloping sides. When the butter is sizzling, pour in ½ the batter and cook 3 to 4 minutes. Loosen the edges of the pancake with a spatula and slide it onto a plate. Invert the pancake back into the skillet and cook about 1 minute until the underside is brown. Invert onto a heating serving plate and keep warm. Prepare the second pancake in the same manner. Sprinkle with powdered sugar. Tear the pancakes into rough pieces with 2 forks and serve immediately.

Makosrétes

Poppy seed strudel

4 servings

- ½ *recipe strudel dough (page 73)*
- ½ *cup milk*
- 1½ *cups ground poppy seeds*
- 4 *tablespoons sugar*
- ½ *cup raisins*
- ¼ *cup apricot preserves*
- 4 *tablespoons melted butter*

Prepare strudel dough and roll it out as directed on page 74. Place the milk, poppy seeds and sugar in a saucepan. Bring to a boil, lower the heat and simmer 15 minutes. Stir in the raisins and preserves and let the mixture cool. Spread the filling on the dough and roll up with the aid of the tea towel. Prick the dough with a fork and brush with butter. Bake in a 350° oven 40 minutes. Let cool before serving.

Streuselkuchen

Streusel cake

6 to 8 servings

- ½ *cup lukewarm milk*
- 1 *package dry yeast*
- ½ *teaspoon salt*
- 2 *tablespoons sugar*
- 2 *eggs, beaten*
- *Grated rind of ½ lemon*
- 6 *tablespoons melted butter*
- 2½ *cups flour*

Streusel topping:

- 1 *cup sugar*
- ¾ *cup butter, softened*
- 1 *teaspoon cinnamon*
- 6 *tablespoons flour*

Combine the milk, yeast, salt and sugar and stir until dissolved. Set aside in a warm place for 10 minutes. Add the eggs and lemon rind. Stir in the butter and flour. Knead the dough until smooth and elastic. Place in a buttered bowl. Cover and let stand in a warm place for 2 hours or until doubled in bulk. Knead for 2 minutes, then roll out on a floured board to form a rectangle ¼ inch thick. Place in a buttered baking tin and let rise for ½ hour. Combine the sugar, butter, cinnamon and flour until crumbly. Sprinkle on top of dough and bake in a preheated 375° oven for 40 minutes.

Zürcher Pfarrhaustorte

Vicarage pie

6 servings

- 1 *cup flour*
- ¼ *teaspoon salt*
- 5 *tablespoons butter, cut in small pieces*
- 2 *to 3 tablespoons water*
- 1 *teaspoon vinegar*
- ½ *cup ground almonds or filberts*
- 1 *egg*
- 1 *teaspoon cinnamon*
- 5 *tablespoons sugar*
- 1 *apple, grated*
- 4 *apples, peeled, cored and sliced into circles*
- ½ *cup blackberry jelly*
- 1 *tablespoon water*

Sift the flour into a bowl. Add the salt and the butter. Blend the butter into the flour using a pastry blender or fingertips. Stir in the water and vinegar, 1 tablespoon at a time, and mix to form a soft dough. Refrigerate for 1 hour. Roll out the dough on a lightly floured board and fit it into a 9 inch pie plate. Combine the almonds, egg, cinnamon, sugar and grated apple and fill the pastry shell. Cover with circles of sliced apple. Heat the blackberry jelly with 1 tablespoon water and pour over the apples. Bake in a preheated 350° oven for 40 to 45 minutes.

Urner Bauernpastete

Farmers pie from Uri

6 to 8 servings

- 4 *cups flour*
- 2 *sticks (8 ounces) butter, cut into small pieces*
- 1 *cup sugar*
- 1 *teaspoon salt*
- 3 *tablespoons Kirsch*
- 1 *egg yolk*
- 1 *teaspoon baking powder*
- ½ *cup grape juice or apple juice*
- 1½ *cups raisins*
- 1 *teaspoon cinnamon*
- 1 *egg yolk, beaten*

Place the flour in a bowl. Add the butter, sugar, salt, Kirsch, egg yolk and baking powder. With the fingertips, combine all these ingredients to form a smooth dough. Chill the dough for 1 hour. Cut in half and roll into two 8 inch squares. Place 1 square on a buttered cookie sheet. Heat the fruit juice, add the raisins and simmer until the liquid is absorbed. Spread the raisins over the pastry. Sprinkle with cinnamon and top with the remaining pastry. Seal the edges securely and brush the surface with beaten egg yolk. Bake in a preheated 350° oven for 45 minutes.

Tiroler Scheiterhaufen

Tyrolean bread and butter pudding

6 servings

- 6 *slices firm textured white bread, crusts removed*
- 2 *tablespoons butter*
- 4 *tart apples, peeled, cored and sliced*
- 1 *tablespoon raisins, soaked in warm water and drained*
- 1 *tablespoon currants, soaked in warm water and drained*
- ¼ *cup sugar*
- 2 *teaspoons cinnamon*
- 4 *egg yolks, lightly beaten*
- 2 *cups milk*

Butter the bread and cut into strips. Arrange a layer of bread in a small buttered casserole. Top with a layer of apples, raisins and currants. Sprinkle with some of the sugar and cinnamon. Repeat the layers until all the ingredients are used. Combine the egg yolks and milk with a wire whisk and pour over the ingredients in the casserole. Bake in a 350° oven 30 to 40 minutes until the top is brown and the custard is set. Let cool to room temperature before serving.

Almas Pite

Apple pie

6 servings

Shortcrust pastry:

- 2½ *cups sifted all purpose flour*
- ½ *teaspoon salt*
- 6 *tablespoons butter, cut into small pieces*
- 6 *tablespoons margerine*
- 6 *tablespoons cold water*

Filling:

- ½ *cup apricot preserves*
- ¼ *cup ground almonds*
- 6 *medium sized cooking apples, peeled, cored and chopped*
- ⅓ *cup sugar*
- *Grated rind and juice of 1 lemon*
- 1 *egg yolk, beaten*
- 2 *tablespoons powdered sugar*

Sift the flour into a bowl. Add the salt, butter and margarine. Blend the butter and margerine into the flour using a pastry blender or fingertips. When thoroughly mixed, add the water. Stir with a fork until the mixture forms a smooth dough. Chill 20 minutes. Cut the pastry in half and roll out to fit an 8 inch pie plate. Spread with apricot preserves and sprinkle on the almonds. Combine the apples, sugar and lemon juice and transfer to the pie shell. Top with the remaining pastry and pinch the edges together. Prick the surface with a fork. Brush with beaten egg yolk and bake in a preheated 375° oven for 45 minutes. Sprinkle with powdered sugar and serve hot or cold.

Mohr im Hemd

Moor in his shirt

6 servings

- 9 *tablespoons butter*
- 10 *tablespoons sugar*
- 8 *slices firm-textured white bread, crusts removed*
- 10 *tablespoons heavy cream*
- 9 *eggs*
- 4 *egg yolks*
- 1 *(6 ounce) package slivered blanched almonds, finely ground*
- 4 *ounces semi-sweet chocolate, melted*
- 1 *cup heavy cream*
- ¼ *cup sugar*

Beat the butter until creamy. Add the sugar gradually, beating constantly until light and fluffy. Soak the bread in the cream. Crumble and beat into the butter mixture. Add the eggs and egg yolks 1 at a time, beating well after each addition. Add the almonds and melted chocolate and beat until well blended. Transfer the mixture to a buttered 2 quart mold. Place in a pan of simmering water to come halfway up the sides of the mold. Cover and cook over low heat 45 minutes. Remove the mold from the pan and let cool completely. Invert the pudding onto a serving plate and chill 1 hour. Beat the 1 cup cream until thick. Add the sugar and beat until stiff. Decorate the pudding with the whipped cream before serving.

Vienna is not the only city famous for its pastry. The Austrian city of Linz, on the Donau, has its own namesake.

Linzer Torte

Cake from Linz

12 servings

Dough:

1 *cup butter, softened*
1⅔ *cups flour*
½ *cup sugar*
½ *cup finely ground almonds*
½ *cup breadcrumbs*
2 *teaspoons powdered cinnamon*
1 *teaspoon finely ground cloves*
Grated rind of ½ lemon
Grated rind of ½ orange
1 *tablespoon rum*
1 *egg*
¼ *teaspoon salt*

Filling:

1 *cup raspberry preserves*
1 *egg, lightly beaten*

Combine all the ingredients for the dough in a mixing bowl and mix to form a smooth dough. Line a 9 inch buttered cake pan with ¾ of the dough so that the sides are ¾ inch high. Fill the center with the preserves. Brush with egg, and bake in a preheated 350° oven for 1 hour. Leave to cool in the cake pan. Unmold and serve.

Sublime in its simplicity is the world-famous 'Sachertorte', which is eaten with only a little half-whipped cream, (recipe page 86, 1st column).

In 1815, when the monarchs and diplomats of all of Europe met at Vienna to re-draw the map of Europe after Napoleon's defeat, Metternich, the Austrian Minister, employed a promising young cook and pastry maker, Franz Sacher. In those times, diplomats believed as much in dinners and feasts as in conferences, and the Congress of Vienna was spent more on the dance floor than in the conference room. For one of Metternich's balls Sacher devised a magnificent creation, sublime and simple: a chocolate cake filled with apricot jam and covered with chocolate icing. This rich dessert was eventually to be called the Sachertorte. Later, when Sacher was older and wiser, he left Metternich's kitchens and opened a restaurant behind the Vienna Opera House. It was here that his creation became famous, mostly through the efforts of his daughter-in-law, Anna Sacher, who ran the restaurant for years, catering to the aristocracy of the Austro-Hungarian Empire. When her pastry chef deserted to a rival and started to bake Sachertortes there, Anna did not hesitate one moment in taking the matter to court, where she won. Since then, pastries bearing the name Sachertorte can only be baked in the Sacher restaurant. They are shipped in wooden crates to all parts of the world as friendly greetings from elegant Vienna, where people know what a good life-and a good pastry- are.

Sachertorte

Cake from Sacher

Cake:

4 ounces semi-sweet chocolate
½ cup butter
1 cup sugar
1 teaspoon vanilla
6 eggs, separated
1¼ cups flour

Glaze:

½ cup apricot preserves

Frosting:

5 ounces semi-sweet chocolate
¼ cup water
2 cups powdered sugar

Place the chocolate in a small saucepan and melt over very low heat, stirring constantly. Set aside to cool. Beat the butter until creamy. Add the sugar gradually and continue beating until the mixture is light and fluffy. Beat in the melted chocolate and vanilla. Add the egg yolks 1 at a time, beating well after each addition. Beat the egg whites until stiff and stir ¼ of the whites into the cake batter. Spoon the remaining egg whites on top of the batter, sprinkle on the flour and carefully fold these ingredients together just until the flour is incorporated. Transfer the batter to a well buttered and floured 9 inch spring form pan and bake in a 350° oven 1 hour. Let the cake cool in the pan. Split the cake into 2 layers and place 1 layer on a serving plate. Melt the apricot preserves over low heat and force through a strainer. Brush the layer with preserves and place the second layer on top. Brush the top and sides of the cake with the remaining preserves. To prepare the frosting, combine the chocolate and water in a saucepan and stir over low heat until the chocolate dissolves. Add the sugar gradually and stir until the mixture is smooth and shiny. Spread the frosting over the top and sides of the cake while still warm.

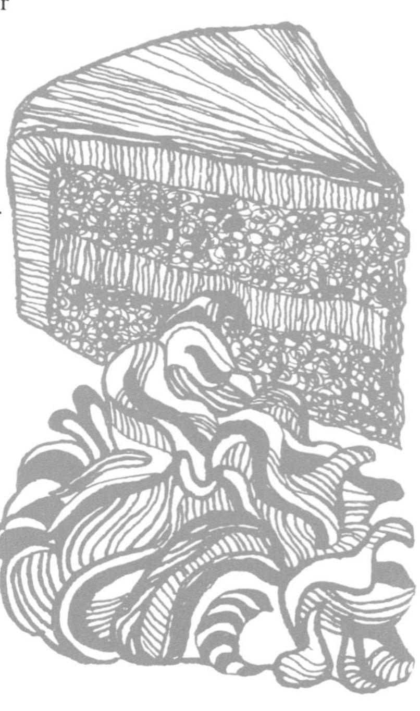

Dobostorta

Dobos cake

Cake:

4 eggs
½ cup sugar
¾ cup flour
Pinch of salt

Filling:

½ cup sugar
6 egg yolks
½ pound sweet butter
6 ounces dark sweet chocolate, melted and cooled

Caramel:

½ cup sugar
¼ cup water

Beat the eggs and sugar together until very thick. Do not underbeat. Sift together the flour and salt and fold gently but thoroughly into the egg mixture. Butter and flour the *outside* bottom of five 8 inch cake tins. Spread a portion of the batter on each, making sure they are evenly covered. Bake in a 375° oven about 7 minutes. Do not overbake. Carefully remove the thin layers from the cake pans with the aid of a spatula and let cool on wire racks. To prepare the filling, combine the sugar and egg yolks in a small heavy saucepan. Cook over low heat, beating constantly with a wire whisk until the mixture is very thick and custard-like. Remove from the heat and cool to room temperature. Beat the butter until light and fluffy. Beat in the egg mixture and the chocolate gradually. Place the most perfect cake layer on an oiled cookie sheet. Combine the sugar and water in a saucepan and simmer without stirring until the mixture is a golden brown. Watch carefully so the caramel does not burn. Dip the bottom of the saucepan into cold water to stop the cooking. Immediately pour the caramel evenly over the cake layer on the cookie sheet. When the caramel is just at the point of setting, mark off 8 triangles with a very sharp oiled knife. Place 1 of the remaining layers on a cake plate and spread with the filling. Continue layering, using the caramel coated layer as the top. Spread the remaining filling on the sides of the cake. This is best made the day before you plan to serve it.

Note: If you do not have 5 cake pans, prepare cake base as directed but bake the layers 1 at a time, letting the batter stand at room temperature while each layer is baking.

Solothurner Nusskuchen

Filbert pie from Solothurn

10 servings

Cake:

6 eggs
1 cup sugar
1 cup flour
2 tablespoons cornstarch
¼ cup ground filberts
1 teaspoon vanilla
½ cup butter, melted

Meringue:

3 egg whites
⅛ teaspoon salt
⅛ teaspoon cream of tartar
½ teaspoon vanilla
¾ cup sugar
¼ cup ground filberts
1 tablespoon cornstarch

Butter cream:

8 ounces butter
2 egg yolks
1 cup powdered sugar
¼ cup ground filberts
1 teaspoon vanilla
Powdered sugar for decoration

Beat the eggs and sugar at high speed in an electric mixer for at least 10 minutes until they are very thick and have doubled in bulk. Sift together the flour, cornstarch and filberts. Add the vanilla to the melted butter. Fold the flour mixture into the egg yolks alternately with the butter mixture. Fold very gently with a spatula to keep as much air as possible in the cake batter. Butter and flour a 9 inch spring form cake pan. Knock out the excess flour and pour the batter into the pan. Bake in a preheated 350° oven for 20 to 25 minutes until golden. Allow the cake to stand for 5 minutes. Unmold and cool on a wire rack.
To prepare the meringue, place the egg whites, salt, cream of tartar and vanilla in a bowl. Beat until the egg whites stand in soft peaks. Add the sugar gradually, beating constantly until stiff peaks are formed. Combine the filberts and cornstarch and fold them carefully into the meringue.
Line 2 cookie sheets with baking paper or brown paper. Draw 2 (9 inch) circles on the paper and divide the meringue evenly between the circles. Smooth the top of the meringue with a spatula. Place in a preheated 275° oven for 1 hour. Do not open the oven door. Turn off the heat and leave the meringue to dry in the oven for 1 more hour. Peel the circles from the paper while they are still warm.
To prepare the butter cream, beat the butter until it is soft and creamy. Beat in the egg yolks and add the powdered sugar gradually. Fold in the nuts and vanilla.
To assemble the cake, place a circle of meringue on a cake plate. Cover with a thin layer of butter cream. Place the cake on the cream and cover with another thin layer of butter cream. Top with the remaining meringue circle. Spread the remaining butter cream around the sides. Dust the top meringue layer heavily with powdered sugar. Chill the cake until ready to serve.
This seems like a fairly complicated cake, but each step is quite easy and the result is worth every minute.

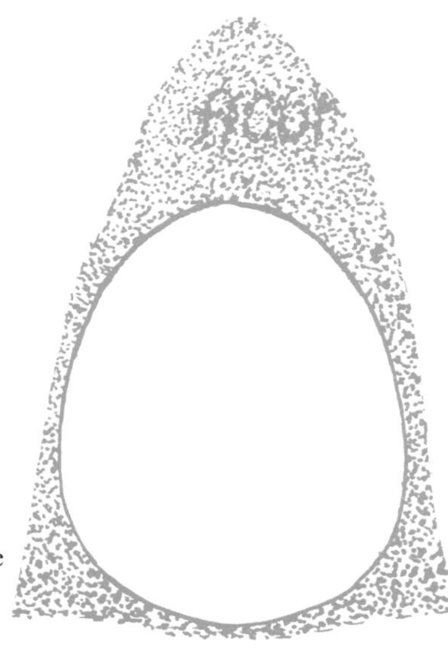

Lusta torta

Lazy cake

10 to 12 servings

½ pound unsalted butter, softened
4 egg yolks
1 cup sugar
1 cup ground almonds
¼ teaspoon almond extract
½ cup rum
½ cup milk
3 packages (48) lady fingers
1 cup heavy cream
2 tablespoons sugar
1 teaspoon vanilla

Beat the butter in a mixer at high speed until light and fluffy. Beat together the egg yolks and sugar until very thick and lemon colored. Combine the egg yolks and sugar with the butter.
Fold in the almonds and almond extract. Pour the rum and milk into a small bowl. Cut the lady fingers in half lengthwise. Dip lady fingers briefly into rum and milk. Do not soak them in the liquid. Line the bottom and sides of an 8 or 9 inch cake pan with lady fingers. Cover with a layer of almond cream. Continue layering dipped lady fingers and almond cream until all are used. Top with a layer of lady fingers. Cover with a clean towel and weight the cake with a plate. Chill for 12 hours. Unmold the cake.
Whip the cream until thickened slightly. Add the sugar and vanilla and continue beating until cream is very thick. Spread the cream attractively over the top and sides of the cake. Decorate the cake with strawberries.

In the Swiss canton of Thurgau, the apple slices are arranged to stand up in the tart.

Thurgauer Apfeltorte

Apple cake from Thurgau

½ cup butter
⅔ cup sugar
2 eggs, separated
Juice of ½ lemon
2 cups sifted flour
2 teaspoons baking powder
¼ teaspoon salt
4 tart apples, peeled, cored and halved
2 tablespoons sugar

In a bowl, beat the butter until creamy. Add the sugar and continue beating until the mixture is light and fluffy. Add the egg yolks 1 at a time, beating well after each addition. Beat in the lemon juice. Beat the egg whites until stiff. Sift together the sifted flour, baking powder and salt. Add the egg whites and flour mixture alternately, mixing only enough to combine the ingredients. Spread the batter in a buttered and floured 9 inch spring form cake pan. Slice the apple halves crosswise into fan-like shapes, leaving the slices attached at the bottom. Arrange the "fans" on top of the batter, pressing them into the dough. Sprinkle the cake with sugar and bake in a 350° oven about 50 minutes or until it tests done. Let cool 10 minutes before slicing. This makes an excellent coffee cake.

St. Galler Klostertorte

Monastery pie from St. Gallen

6 to 8 servings

2 cups flour
1 teaspoon baking powder
8 tablespoons butter, cut into small pieces
½ cup ground almonds
1 teaspoon cinnamon
½ cup sugar
2 to 3 tablespoons milk
1 cup blackberry preserves
1 egg yolk, beaten

Combine the flour, baking powder, butter, almonds, cinnamon and sugar with a pastry blender or the finger tips. Add the milk and stir with a fork to form a smooth dough. Refrigerate for 1 hour. Roll out ¾ of the dough and fit into a buttered and floured 8 inch spring form tart tin. Cut the remainder of the pastry into long strips. Lay one strip in a circle around the sides of the pastry. Fill the shell with preserves and lay a criss cross pattern of pastry strips on top. Brush with egg yolk and bake in a preheated 350° oven for 40 minutes. Cool and serve.

Tarte aux poires à la Genevoise

Pie with pears from Geneva

6 to 8 servings

1 9 inch unbaked pie shell (use 1 package frozen patty shells, thawed and rolled into a circle)
1 tablespoon flour
2 tablespoons sugar
1 teaspoon cinnamon
6 ripe pears
½ teaspoon grated lemon rind
½ teaspoon grated orange rind
¼ cup raisins
2 to 3 tablespoons dry white wine
2 tablespoons oil
2 to 3 tablespoons sugar
½ cup heavy cream

Line a 9 inch pie plate with the pastry and prick with a fork. Combine the flour, sugar and cinnamon and sprinkle on top of the pastry. Peal the pears and cut each pear in half. Remove the cores and arrange the pears cut side down on the pastry. Cut the pears into slices, cutting almost all the way through but keeping the slices still joined together. Sprinkle the pears with lemon rind, orange rind and raisins. Combine the wine and oil and pour over the pears. Top with sugar and cream. Place in a preheated 400° oven and bake for 10 minutes. Reduce the heat to 350° and bake for another 25 minutes.

Weintorte

Wine cake

Cake:
7 eggs, separated
1⅓ cups sugar
Grated rind of 1 lemon
2 tablespoons rum
1 cup plus 2 tablespoons ground almonds
1 cup plus 2 tablespoons fine dry breadcrumbs
Pinch of salt

Topping:
1 cup red wine
½ cup sugar
¼ teaspoon cinnamon
¼ teaspoon ground cloves

Butter a 9 inch spring form cake pan and dust with fine dry breadcrumbs. Beat the egg yolks with the sugar until very thick. Do not underbeat. Gradually add the lemon rind, rum, almonds and breadcrumbs, beating just until the dry ingredients are incorporated. Beat the egg whites with a pinch of salt until stiff peaks form. Stir ⅓ of the whites into the batter, making sure the ingredients are thoroughly combined. Carefully fold in the remaining whites and transfer the batter to the prepared cake pan. Bake in a 275° oven 1 to 1¼ hours, until a cake tester comes out clean. Meanwhile, place the wine, sugar, cinnamon and cloves in a saucepan and stir over low heat until the sugar dissolves. When the cake is done, pour the wine mixture over it. Remove from the pan and serve warm or cold.

Túróslepény

Cottage cheese pie

1 pound cottage cheese
6 tablespoons sugar
1 teaspoon vanilla
Juice and grated rind of 1 lemon
5 eggs, separated
1 cup raisins
1 recipe short crust pastry (page 67)
2 tablespoons powdered sugar

In a bowl, combine the cottage cheese, sugar, vanilla, lemon juice and rind. Add the egg yolks 1 at a time, beating well after each addition. Stir in the raisins. Beat the egg whites until stiff and gently fold into the cottage cheese mixture. Roll out ½ the pastry and line a deep pie plate with it. Add the cottage cheese mixture. Roll out the remaining pastry and cover the filling, pinching the edges of the pastry together to seal. Prick the top crust with a fork and bake the pie in a 350° oven 45 minutes. Sprinkle with powdered sugar and let cool completely before serving.

Faschingskrapfen

Carnivals fritters

1 package dry yeast
½ cup lukewarm milk
6 tablespoons sugar
3 to 3½ cups flour
4 egg yolks
1 egg
½ teaspoon salt
½ cup butter, melted and cooled
3 tablespoons rum
Grated rind of 1 lemon
½ cup marmalade
Oil for deep frying

Sprinkle the yeast over the lukewarm milk and stir to dissolve. Add 1 tablespoon sugar and ½ cup flour and beat until smooth. Cover and let stand in a warm place ½ hour. Beat the egg yolks and egg with the remaining sugar until foamy. Add the salt, butter, rum and and lemon rind and combine thoroughly. Beat in the yeast mixture. Add the remaining flour, ½ cup at a time, until the dough begins to pull away from the sides of the bowl. Turn it out onto a floured board and knead until very smooth and elastic, using more flour as necessary to prevent sticking. Place the dough in an oiled bowl. Cover and let rise 1 hour or until doubled in bulk. Turn the dough out onto a floured board and knead 1 minute. Roll it out to a ½ inch thickness and cut into 2 to 2½ inch rounds with a cookie cutter. Spread half the rounds with marmalade and top with the remaining rounds. Pinch the edges together with wet fingers to seal. Cover and let stand 30 minutes. Heat the oil for deep frying and fry the fritters a few at a time until golden brown. Drain on paper towels and serve warm.

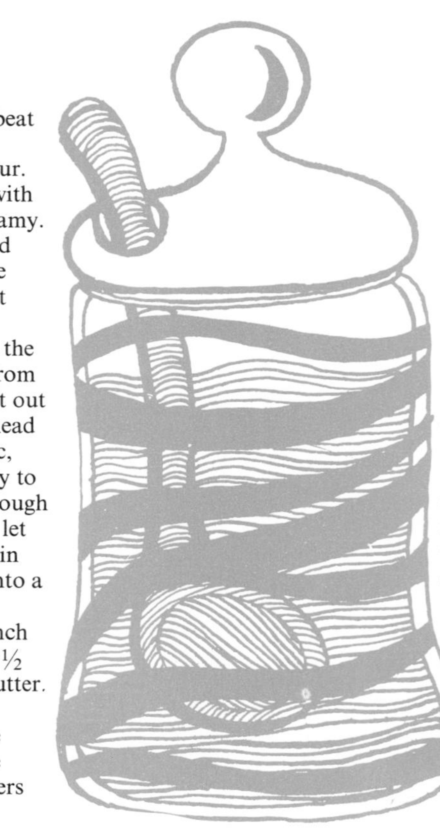

Palacsinta

mistake

Hungarian panckaes

20 5 to 6 inch pancakes

1¼ cups flour
2 eggs
1 egg yolk
¾ cup milk
½ cup water
1 tablespoon sugar
Pinch of salt
2 tablespoons melted butter

Place the flour, eggs, egg yolk, milk, water, sugar, salt and 1 tablespoon butter in a blender. Blend at high speed until the batter is smooth. Scrape down the sides of the blender if the flour sticks and blend again. Heat a 5½ inch crêpe pan or other small skillet. Add the remaining butter and heat until the foam subsides. Tip out the butter and add a spoonful of batter, rolling it around to coat the bottom evenly. Tip out the excess batter and cook over high heat several seconds until the pancake is golden brown. Turn and cook a few seconds on the other side. Discard the first pancake which will be oily. Continue cooking the pancakes in this manner until all the batter is used. Spread each pancake with jam or honey and raisins and roll up. Serve immediately.

Müesli

Müesli

4 servings

- *4 tablespoons oatmeal*
- *1 cup water*
- *4 tablespoons lemon juice*
- *4 tablespoons condensed milk*
- *6 medium sized apples, unpeeled and grated*
- *4 tablespoons chopped filberts or almonds*

Soak the oatmeal in the water for 12 hours. Add the lemon juice, condensed milk and grated apples. Sprinkle chopped filberts or almonds over the müesli.
This is the basic preparation but there are many variations. Omit the apples and add strawberries, other berries or finely chopped apricots or prunes. Two other good combinations are sliced apples and bananas and sliced apples and oranges or mandarin oranges. The condensed milk can be replaced with ¾ cup yogurt and 4 tablespoons of honey. Other cereals may be substituted for the oatmeal. Müesli is not, in fact, a dessert but can be eaten as a first course at any meal.
In Switzerland the dish is popular both as a breakfast dish or for a snack.

Mandelsuppe

Almond soup

4 servings

- *2 teaspoons cornstarch*
- *2 cups milk*
- *½ cup blanched, chopped almonds*
- *2 egg yolks*
- *1 cup cream*
- *½ cup sugar*
- *¼ teaspoon cinnamon*

Stir the cornstarch into 1 tablespoon of the milk. Heat the remaining milk in a saucepan. Add the almonds, reduce the heat and simmer gently for ½ hour. Beat the egg yolks lightly. Add the cream and beat until thickened. Add the sugar and cinnamon and beat until stiff. Add the cornstarch paste to the hot milk, stirring constantly. Stir in the cream and serve hot.

Marillensuppe

Apricot soup

4 servings

- *½ pound fresh apricots*
- *2 tablespoons sugar*
- *4 cups water*
- *1 tablespoon cornstarch dissolved in 2 tablespoons cold water*
- *Juice of 1 lemon*

Peel and remove the pits from the apricots. Place the sugar in a saucepan. Add the water and bring to boiling point. Add the apricots and simmer for 30 minutes. Remove the apricots from the syrup and cool slightly. Force the apricots through a strainer. Return the apricot purée to the pan with the syrup. Stir in the cornstarch paste. Bring to a boil and continue cooking until the soup has thickened. Stir in the lemon juice and serve.

Gesztenyepure

Chestnut purée

4 servings

- *1 (15 ounce) can whole chestnuts, drained*
- *¼ cup milk*
- *¼ cup sugar*
- *½ teaspoon vanilla*
- *1 tablespoon dark rum*
- *¼ cup heavy cream, whipped*

Force the chestnuts through a sieve into a bowl. Combine the milk and sugar in a small saucepan and heat, stirring until the sugar dissolves. Add the milk mixture, vanilla and rum to the chestnuts and combine thoroughly. Chill 2 to 3 hours. Mound the purée on a serving dish and decorate with the whipped cream.

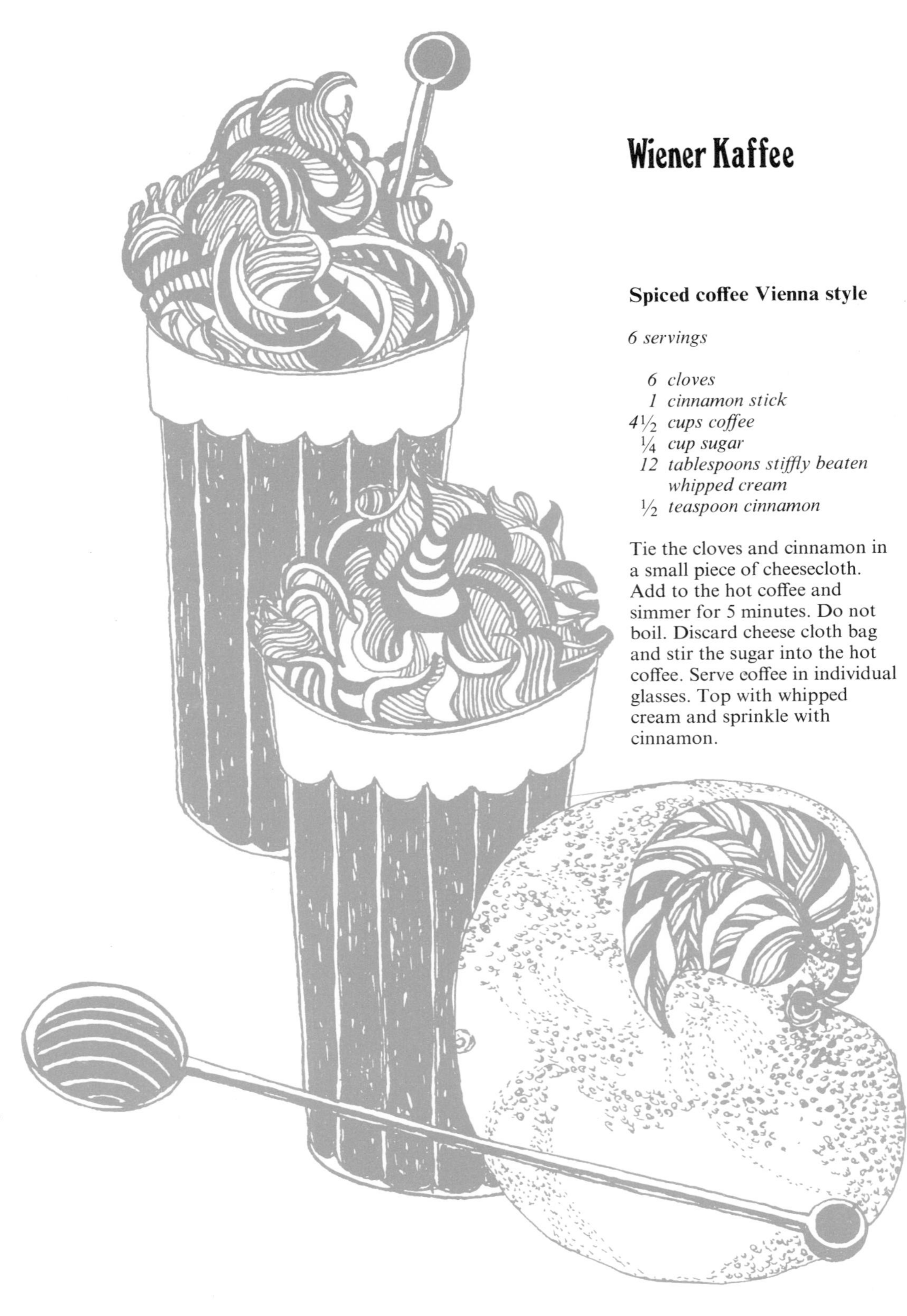

Wiener Kaffee

Of the many ways to prepare it, the simplest is just to add hot milk and sugar to very strong coffee. But most popular is 'Melange mit Schlagobers', strong coffee with hot milk and sugar and a thick glob of whipped cream floating on top. And if it is very cold, you can always order melange with egg: the egg is beaten together with sugar in a glass, then hot coffee is added and finally topped with whipped cream. Viennese women often drink melange made of equal parts of hot coffee and hot chocolate, again, with the inevitable whipped cream topping.

The world would be a less interesting place to live in, with fewer novels, poems, symphonies or operas, if Vienna's coffee houses had never existed. Since the Turks introduced a taste for coffee in the 17th century, the artists, poets and musicians of Vienna have gathered in the large and old-fashioned Viennese coffee houses. These are still an institution almost exclusively for men. Writers and journalists, and businessmen, government officials and lawyers all go there. They take newspapers from a rack and go to sit on leather benches or wooden or straw stools to drink their coffee. Today, this coffee is often the product of an Italian expresso machine. But it always used to be Mokka (strong black coffee) or Melange, served in glass cups with silver holders.

Spiced coffee Vienna style

6 servings

- 6 *cloves*
- 1 *cinnamon stick*
- 4½ *cups coffee*
- ¼ *cup sugar*
- 12 *tablespoons stiffly beaten whipped cream*
- ½ *teaspoon cinnamon*

Tie the cloves and cinnamon in a small piece of cheesecloth. Add to the hot coffee and simmer for 5 minutes. Do not boil. Discard cheese cloth bag and stir the sugar into the hot coffee. Serve coffee in individual glasses. Top with whipped cream and sprinkle with cinnamon.

Kakao mit Schlagobers

Chocolate with whipped cream

4 servings

- 4 *cups milk*
- 4 *tablespoons powdered cocoa*
- 5 *teaspoons sugar*
- ¾ *cup cream*

Bring the milk to a boil, add the cocoa and 3 teaspoons sugar slowly, stirring constantly. Beat the cream with the remaining sugar until stiff. Pour the cocoa into individual cups, top generously with whipped cream and serve immediately.

Glühwein

Wine punch

4 servings

- 2 *cups red wine*
- 8 *sugar cubes*
- 2 *whole cloves*
- 2 *strips lemon rind*
- 1 *teaspoon vanilla*

Place all the ingredients except the vanilla in a small saucepan. Heat, stirring until the sugar dissolves. Continue to heat the mixture until it is very hot but do not let it boil. Stir in the vanilla. Strain into small heated mugs and serve.

Kardinal

Cardinal

6 servings

- 5 *sugar cubes*
- 1 *orange*
- 1 *cup pineapple juice*
- ½ *bottle sweet white wine*
- ½ *bottle demi-sec Champagne*

Rub the sugar cubes over the orange peel and place in a glass pitcher. Squeeze the orange and add the juice to the sugar. Stir the sugar and orange juice together until the sugar is dissolved. Stir in the pineapple juice and white wine. Cover and refrigerate 2 hours. When ready to serve, add a few ice cubes and the Champagne.

Eierbier

Egg beer

4 servings

- 4 *cups beer (1 quart)*
- 8 *cubes sugar, soaked in*
  2 tablespoons lemon juice
- 4 *egg yolks*

Combine the beer with the sugar cubes soaked in lemon juice. Bring to simmering point but do not boil. Beat the egg yolks with a few tablespoons of cold beer and add to the hot beer. Serve hot.

Kitchen terms

Aspic
A stiff gelatine obtained by combining fish or meat bouillon with gelatine powder.

Au gratin
Obtained by covering a dish with a white sauce (usually prepared with grated cheese) and then heating the dish in the oven so that a golden crust forms.

Baste
To moisten meat or other foods while cooking to add flavor and to prevent drying of the surface. The liquid is usually melted fat, meat drippings, fruit juice or sauce.

Blanch (precook)
To preheat in boiling water or steam. (1) Used to inactivate enzymes and shrink food for canning, freezing, and drying. Vegetables are blanched in boiling water or steam, and fruits in boiling fruit juice, sirup, water, or steam. (2) Used to aid in removal of skins from nuts, fruits, and some vegetables.

Blend
To mix thoroughly two or more ingredients.

Fold
To combine by using two motions, cutting vertically through the mixture and turning over and over by sliding the implement across the bottom of the mixing bowl with each turn.

Fry
To cook in fat; applied especially (1) to cooking in a small amount of fat, also called sauté or pan-fry; (2) to cooking in a deep layer of fat, also called deep-fat frying.

Marinate
To let food stand in a marinade usually an oil–acid mixture like French dressing.

Parboil
To boil until partially cooked. The cooking is usually completed by another method.

Poach
To cook in a hot liquid using precautions to retain shape. The temperature used varies with the food.

Roast
To cook, uncovered, by dry heat. Usually done in an oven, but occasionally in ashes, under coals or on heated stones or metals. The term is usually applied to meats but may refer to other food as potatoes, corn, chestnuts.

Sauté
To brown or cook in a small amount of fat. See Fry.

Simmer
To cook in a liquid just below the boiling point, at temperatures of 185°–210° Bubbles form slowly and collapse below the surface.

Alphabetical index

English

79 Almond crescents
91 Almond soup (Austria)
83 Apple pie (Hungary)
89 Apple pie from Thurgau (Switzerland)
80 Apple strudel (Austria)
78 Apricot dumplings (Austria)
91 Apricot soup (Austria)

58 Bacon and apple stew (Switzerland)
75 Baked corn (Rumania)
59 Barbecued sausages (Rumania)
25 Beef broth with semolina dumplings (Austria)
24 Beef soup from Vienna (Austria)
50 Beef with gherkins (Czechoslovakia)
14 Bohemian eggs (Austria)
49 Boiled beef (Austria)
51 Boiled fresh ham (Austria)
51 Bosnian black pot (Yugoslavia)
26 Bread dumplings (Austria)
21 Bread soup with eggs (Austria)

22 Cabbage soup (Switzerlamd)
73 Cabbage stuffed strudel (Austria)
84 Cake from Linz (Austria)
86 Cake from Sacher (Austria)
46 Calves' liver paprika (Hungary)
43 Caraway goulash (Austria)
23 Caraway seed soup (Czechoslovakia)
93 Cardinal (Austria)
90 Carnivals fritters (Hungary)
31 Carp in black sauce (Czechoslovakia)
30 Carp in red wine (Austria)
28 Carp soup (Hungary)
30 Carp stew (Hungary)
31 Carp with sour cream (Austria)
74 Carrot cake from Aargau (Switzerland)
17 Cheese fondue (Switzerland)
18 Cheese fritters (Austria)
17 Cheese pie from Fribourg (Switzerland)
13 Cheese sandwiches from Solothurn (Switzerland)
24 Cheese soup (Switzerland)
17 Cheese steak (Switzerland)
91 Chestnut purée (Hungary)
63 Chicken Bacska style (Hungary)
63 Chicken in sour cream (Hungary)
65 Chicken in wine sauce (Switzerland)
63 Chicken ragout (Austria)
20 Chicken soup with liver dumplings (Austria)
61 Chicken stew (Rumania)
62 Chicken stew (Austria)
93 Chocolate with whipped cream (Austria)
34 Cold trout (Austria)
15 Cottage cheese spread (Hungary)
90 Cottage cheese pie (Hungary)
58 Counselor's stew Zurich (Switzerland)
78 Cream cheese crescents (Austria)
20 Creamed liver soup (Austria)
78 Crescent rolls (Austria)
23 Cucumber soup (Austria)

86 Dobos cake (Austria)
66 Duck and red cabbage (Czechoslovakia)

66 Duck with sweet corn (Rumania)

93 Egg beer (Austria)
75 Eggplant salad (Rumania)
12 Eggs Tyrolean style (Austria)
82 Emperor's pancake (Austria)

83 Farmers pie from Uri (Switzerland)
87 Filbert pie from Solothurn (Switzerland)
14 Filled eggs (Austria)
48 Fillet of veal Vienna style (Austria)
38 Fish and mushrooms (Hungary)
39 Fish in foil (Rumania)
21 Fish soup (Hungary)
36 Fish stew (Austria)
39 Fish with asparagus (Austria)
39 Flounder fillets (Austria)
32 Fried carp (Austria)
66 Fried chicken (Austria)

41 Goulash (Hungary)
43 Goulash Klausenburg style (Hungary)
19 Goulash soup (Hungary)
41 Goulash with pickled cucumbers (Austria)

27 Ham patches (Austria)
38 Herring fillets Bohemian style (Czechoslovakia)
78 Honey cookies (Switzerland)
90 Hungarian pancakes (Hungary)

21 Lamb soup (Hungary)
49 Larded veal birds (Austria)
87 Lazy cake (Hungary)
71 Leek dish from Vaud (Switzerland)
27 Liver dumplings (Austria)
59 Liver patties Neuenburg (Switzerland)

81 Marmor cake (Austria)
55 Meat and sauerkraut Bern style (Switzerland)
59 Meat patties (Rumania)
60 Meat pie from Chur (Switzerland)
15 Meat salad (Austria)
43 Meat stew with sour cream (Hungary)
89 Monastery pie from St. Galler (Switzerland)
83 Moor in his shirt (Austria)
91 Müesli (Switzerland)
75 Mushrooms and asparagus salad (Hungary)
23 Mushroom soup (Czechoslovakia)

27 Noodle pie (Austria)
79 Nut crescents (Austria)

18 Omelet from the Jura (Switzerland)
74 Onion pie from Schaffhausen (Switzerland)

29 Paprika carp (Austria)
63 Paprika chicken (Hungary)
19 Paprika soup (Hungary)
23 Paradise soup (Austria)
22 Pea soup with pork (Austria)
72 Peppers and tomatoes (Austria)
89 Pie with pears from Geneva (Switzerland)
35 Pike in caper sauce (Austria)
38 Pike or perch Keszthely (Hungary)
26 Plain noodle dough (Austria)
77 Plum dumplings (Austria)
82 Poppy seed strudel (Hungary)
43 Pork and cabbage stew (Austria)
47 Pork Appenzell style (Switzerland)
52 Pork chops with sauerkraut (Austria)
42 Pork goulash (Hungary)
54 Pork hocks Geneva style (Switzerland)
47 Pork stew from Stiermarken (Austria)
42 Pork with rice (Austria)
26 Potato dumplings (Austria)
27 Potato dumplings, Aargau style (Austria)
74 Potato pancake (Switzerland)
74 Potato paprika (Hungary)
15 Potato salad (Austria)
24 Potato soup (Czechoslovakia)
21 Potato soup Vienna style (Austria)

67 Rabbit pie (Austria)
67 Rabbit Ticino style (Switzerland)
75 Red beet salad (Hungary)
69 Rice with green beans (Hungary)
55 Roast beef Gypsy style (Hungary)
66 Roast duckling (Austria)
67 Roast goose (Austria)
56 Roast leg of lamb (Austria)
14 Rolled eggs (Austria)

62 Sacher chicken (Austria)
31 Salmon Basler style (Switzerland)
33 Salmon Ticino style (Switzerland)
24 Sauerkraut soup (Hungary)
46 Shredded liver Thurgau style (Switzerland)
44 Shredded veal Zurich style (Switzerland)
77 Snow balls (Austria)
92 Spiced coffee Vienna style (Austria)
71 Spinach dumplings (Switzerland)
22 Spinach soup from Aargau (Switzerland)
50 Steak Esterházy (Hungary)
47 Stewed pork (Hungary)
57 Stew from Fribourg (Switzerland)
82 Streusel cake (Hungary)
59 Stuffed cabbage with sauerkraut (Hungary)
35 Stuffed fillets Vienna style (Austria)
70 Stuffed onions (Switzerland)
69 Stuffed peppers (Austria)
35 Stuffed pike or perch (Austria)
70 Stuffed sauerkraut (Rumania)
46 Stuffed veal (Austria)

50 Transylvanian stew (Rumania)
34 Trout with tomato and bacon (Austria)
83 Tyrolean bread and butter pudding (Austria)
34 Tyrolean trout (Austria)

48 Veal cutlets Emmental style (Switzerland)
54 Veal ragout (Austria)
54 Veal stew (Czechoslovakia)
53 Veal tongue (Austria)

82 Vicarage pie (Switzerland)
71 Viennese cauliflower (Austria)

89 Wine cake (Switzerland)
93 Wine punch (Austria)

Foreign languages:

27 Aargauer Kartoffelpfluten (Switzerland)
74 Aargauer Rüeblitorte (Switzerland)
22 Aargauer Spinatsuppe (Switzerland)
83 Almas Pite (Hungary)
80 Apfelstrudel (Austria)
47 Appenzellerli (Switzerland)

66 Backhendl (Austria)
21 Bárány leves (Hungary)
55 Berner Platte (Switzerland)
14 Böhmer Eierspeise (Austria)
51 Bosnische schwarze Pfanne (Yugoslavia)
24 Bramborova polevka (Czechoslovakia)
21 Brotsuppe mit Eiern (Austria)
79 Buchteln (Austria)
74 Burgunya paprikás (Hungary)

59 Chifteluta (Rumania)
60 Churer Fleischtorte (Switzerland)
67 Coniglio arrosto alla ticinese (Switzerland)
63 Csirke bácska (Hungary)
63 Csirke tejfolben (Hungary)

86 Dobostorta (Hungary)

93 Eierbier (Austria)
62 Eingemachtes Huhn (Austria)
54 Eingemachtes Kalbsfleisch (Austria)
48 Emmenthaler Schnitzel (Switzerland)
22 Erbsensuppe mit Schweinefleisch (Austria)
50 Eszterházy rostélyos (Hungary)

90 Faschingskrapfen (Austria)
35 Fischfilets nach Wiener Art (Austria)
39 Fisch mit Spargeln (Austria)
36 Fischragout (Austria)
17 Fondue (Switzerland)
34 Forellen mit Paradiesäpfeln (Austria)

17 Gâteau au fromage Fribourgeoise (Switzerland)
32 Gebackener Karpfen (Austria)
67 Gebratene Gans (Austria)
66 Gebratenes Entchen (Austria)
14 Gefüllte kalte Eier (Austria)
69 Gefüllte Paprikaschoten (Austria)
70 Gefüllte Zwiebeln (Switzerland)
35 Gefüllter Hecht (Austria)
46 Gefüllter Kalbsbraten (Austria)
51 Gekochter Schweinschlegel (Austria)
14 Gerollte Eierspeise (Austria)
49 Gespickte Kalbsvögerl (Austria)
91 Gesztenyepure (Hungary)
93 Glühwein (Austria)
81 Gugelhupf (Austria)

41 Gulyas (Hungary)
19 Gulyás leves (Hungary)
23 Gurkensuppe (Austria)

21 Hálaszlé (Hungary)
38 Hal gombaval (Hungary)
38 Hal keszthely (Hungary)
56 Hammelkeule (Austria)
35 Hecht in Kapernsauce
38 Heringe Böhmer Art (Czechoslovakia)
78 Honigleckerli (Switzerland)
23 Houbova polevka (Czechoslovakia)
63 Hühnerragout (Austria)
20 Hühnersuppe mit Leberknödel (Austria)

18 Jura Omelette (Switzerland)

22 Kabis Suppe (Switzerland)
66 Kachnas cervenym-zelim (Czechoslovakia)
66 Kacsa kukoricaval (Rumania)
82 Kaiserschmarren (Austria)
93 Kakao mit Schlagobers (Austria)
53 Kalbszunge (Austria)
34 Kalte Forellenfilets (Austria)
67 Kaninchenpastete (Austria)
24 Kaposztaleves (Hungary)
31 Kapr na cerno (Czechoslovakia)
93 Kardinal (Austria)
71 Karfiol Wiener Art (Austria)
30 Karpf im Rotwein (Austria)
31 Karpfen mit saurer Sahne (Austria)
26 Kartoffelknödel (Austria)
15 Kartoffelsalat (Austria)
17 Käse Beignet (Switzerland)
18 Käsekrapfen (Austria)
78 Kipfeln (Austria)

23 Kminova polevka (Czechoslovakia)
43 Koloszvári gulyas (Hungary)
15 Körözött (Hungary)
25 Kraftbrühe mit Griesznockerl (Austria)
43 Krautfleisch (Austria)
73 Krautstrudel (Austria)
43 Kümmelfleisch (Austria)

31 Lachs nach Basler Art (Switzerland)
27 Leberknödel (Austria)
20 Lebersuppe mit Rahm (Austria)
84 Linzer Torte (Austria)
87 Lusta torta (Hungary)

43 Majoran tokany (Hungary)
82 Makosrétes (Hungary)
75 Mamaliga (Rumania)
91 Mandelsuppe (Austria)
78 Marillenknödel (Austria)
91 Marillensuppe (Austria)
59 Mititei (Rumania)
83 Mohr im Hemd (Austria)
91 Müesli (Switzerland)

59 Neuenburger Leberpastetchen (Switzerland)
27 Nudelschöberl (Austria)
26 Nudelteig (Austria)
79 Nusskipfeln (Austria)

90 Palacsinta (Hungary)
71 Papet Vaudois (Switzerland)
29 Paprika Karpfen (Austria)
19 Paprikás leves (Hungary)
63 Paprikás csirke (Hungary)
72 Paprika Tomaten Gemüse (Austria)
23 Paradiessuppe (Austria)
39 Peste al bastru (Rumania)
77 Pflaumenknödel (Austria)

Index by type of dish

54 Pieds de porc (Switzerland)
65 Pollo alla montanara (Switzerland)
28 Ponty leves (Hungary)
30 Pontypörkölt (Austria)
47 Pörkölt (Hungary)
46 Pörkölt Borjumaj (Hungary)
57 Potée Fribourgeoise (Switzerland)
61 Puï Românese (Rumania)

42 Reisfleisch (Austria)
69 Reis mit Bohnen (Austria)
75 Repasaláta (Hungary)
15 Rindfleischsalat (Austria)
55 Rostélyos cigány módra (Hungary)
75 Rösti (Switzerland)

62 Sacher Huhn (Austria)
86 Sachertorte (Austria)
75 Salate de vinete (Rumania)
33 Salmone alla ticinese (Switzerland)
70 Sarmalutsa (Rumania)
74 Schaffhauser Bölletünne (Switzerland)
27 Schinkenfleckern (Austria)
77 Schneenockerl (Austria)
58 Schnitz und drunder (Switzerland)
39 Schollenschnitzel (Austria)
52 Schweinekotelett auf Sauerkraut (Austria)
26 Semmelknödel (Austria)
13 Solothurner Käseschnitte (Switzerland)
87 Solothurner Nusskuchen (Switzerland)
75 Spárgasaláta (Hungary)
71 Spinat Pizokel (Switzerland)
47 Steirisches Wurzelfleisch (Austria)
89 St. Galler Klostertorte (Switzerland)
82 Streuselkuchen (Austria)
42 Székely gulyas (Hungary)

49 Tafelspitz (Austria)
89 Tarte aux poires à la Genevoise (Switzerland)
54 Teleci gulas (Czechoslovakia)
89 Thurgauer Apfeltorte (Switzerland)
46 Thurgauer Leberspätzli (Switzerland)
12 Tiroler Eierspeise (Austria)
34 Tiroler Forellen (Austria)
83 Tiroler Scheiterhaufen (Austria)
50 Tocana (Rumania)
59 Töltött káposzta (Hungary)
78 Topfenkipfeln (Austria)
90 Túróslepény (Hungary)

83 Urner Bauernpastete (Switzerland)
24 Urner Käsesuppe (Switzerland)

89 Weintorte (Switzerland)
92 Wiener Kaffee (Austria)
21 Wiener Fleischsuppe (Austria)
21 Wiener Kraftsuppe (Austria)
48 Wiener Schnitzel (Austria)

41 Znaimer Goulasch (Austria)
50 Znojemska pecene (Czechoslovakia)
44 Zürcher Geschnetzeltes (Switzerland)
82 Zürcher Pfarrhaustorte (Switzerland)
58 Zürcher Ratsherrntopf (Switzerland)

English

Entrees

14 Bohemian eggs (Austria)
13 Cheese sandwiches from Solothurn (Switzerland)
15 Cottage cheese spread (Hungary)
12 Eggs Tyrolean style (Austria)
14 Filled eggs (Austria)
15 Meat salad (Austria)
15 Potato salad (Austria)
14 Rolled eggs (Austria)

Cheese dishes

17 Cheese fondue (Switzerland)
18 Cheese fritters (Austria)
17 Cheese pie from Fribourg (Switzerland)
17 Cheese steak (Switzerland)
18 Omelet from the Jura (Switzerland)

Soups

25 Beef broth with semolina dumplings (Austria)
24 Beef soup from Vienna (Austria)
21 Bread soup with eggs (Austria)
22 Cabbage soup (Switzerland)
23 Caraway seed soup (Czechoslovakia)
24 Cheese soup (Switzerland)
20 Chicken soup with liver dumplings (Austria)
20 Creamed liver soup (Austria)
23 Cucumber soup (Austria)
21 Fish soup (Hungary)
19 Goulash soup (Hungary)
21 Lamb soup (Hungary)
23 Mushroom soup (Czechoslovakia)
19 Paprika soup (Hungary)
23 Paradise soup (Austria)
22 Pea soup with pork (Austria)
24 Potato soup (Czechoslovakia)
21 Potato soup Vienna style (Austria)
24 Sauerkraut soup (Hungary)
22 Spinach soup from Aargau (Switzerland)

Dumplings

26 Bread dumplings (Austria)
27 Ham patches (Austria)
27 Liver dumplings (Austria)
27 Noodle pie (Austria)
26 Plain noodle dough (Austria)
26 Potato dumplings (Austria)
27 Potato dumplings, Aargau style (Austria)

Fish dishes

31 Carp in black sauce (Czechoslovakia)
30 Carp in red wine (Austria)
28 Carp soup (Hungary)
30 Carp stew (Hungary)
31 Carp with sour cream (Austria)
34 Cold trout (Austria)
38 Fish and mushrooms (Hungary)
39 Fish in foil (Rumania)
36 Fish stew (Austria)

39 Fish with asparagus (Austria)
39 Flounder fillets (Austria)
32 Fried carp (Austria)
38 Herring fillets Bohemian style (Czechoslovakia)
29 Paprika carp (Austria)
35 Pike in caper sauce (Austria)
38 Pike or perch Keszthely (Hungary)
31 Salmon Basler style (Switzerland)
33 Salmon Ticino style (Switzerland)
35 Stuffed fillets Vienna style (Austria)
35 Stuffed pike or perch (Austria)
34 Trout with tomato and bacon (Austria)
34 Tyrolean trout (Austria)

Meat dishes

58 Bacon and apple stew (Switzerland)
59 Barbecued sausages (Rumania)
50 Beef with gherkins (Czechoslovakia)
49 Boiled beef (Austria)
51 Boiled fresh ham (Austria)
51 Bosnian black pot (Yugoslavia)
46 Calves' liver paprika (Hungary)
43 Caraway goulash (Austria)
58 Counselor's stew Zurich (Switzerland)
48 Fillet of veal Vienna style (Austria)
41 Goulash (Hungary)
43 Goulash Klausenburg style (Hungary)
41 Goulash with pickled cucumbers (Austria)
49 Larded veal birds (Austria)
59 Liver patties Neuenburg (Switzerland)
55 Meat and sauerkraut Bern style (Switzerland)
59 Meat patties (Rumania)
60 Meat pie from Chur (Switzerland)
43 Meat stew with sour cream (Hungary)
43 Pork and cabbage stew (Austria)
47 Pork Appenzell style (Switzerland)
52 Pork chops with sauerkraut (Austria)
42 Pork goulash (Hungary)
54 Pork hocks Geneva style (Switzerland)
47 Pork stew from Stiermarken(Austria)
42 Pork with rice (Austria)
55 Roast beef Gypsy style (Hungary)
56 Roast leg of lamb (Austria)
46 Shredded liver Thurgau style (Switzerland)
44 Shredded veal Zurich style (Switzerland)
50 Steak Esterházy (Hungary)
47 Stewed pork (Hungary)
57 Stew from Fribourg (Switzerland)
59 Stuffed cabbage with sauerkraut (Hungary)
46 Stuffed veal (Austria)
50 Transylvanian stew (Rumania)
48 Veal cutlets Emmental style (Switzerland)
54 Veal ragout (Austria)
54 Veal stew (Czechoslovakia)
53 Veal tongue (Austria)

Poultry and game dishes

63 Chicken Bacska style (Hungary)
63 Chicken in sour cream (Hungary)
65 Chicken in wine sauce (Switzerland)
63 Chicken ragout (Austria)
61 Chicken stew (Rumania)
62 Chicken stew (Austria)
66 Duck and red cabbage (Czechoslovakia)
66 Duck with sweet corn (Rumania)
66 Fried chicken (Austria)
63 Paprika chicken (Hungary)
67 Rabbit pie (Austria)
67 Rabbit Ticino style (Switzerland)
66 Roast duckling (Austria)
67 Roast goose (Austria)
62 Sacher chicken (Austria)

Vegetable dishes

75 Baked corn (Rumania)
73 Cabbage stuffed strudel (Austria)
74 Carrot cake from Aargau
75 Eggplant salad (Rumania)
71 Leek dish from Vaud (Switzerland)
75 Mushroom and asparagus salad (Hungary)
74 Onion pie from Schaffhausen (Switzerland)
72 Peppers and tomatoes (Austria)
74 Potato pancake (Switzerland)
74 Potato paprika (Hungary)
75 Red beet salad (Hungary)
69 Rice with green beans (Hungary)
71 Spinach dumplings (Switzerland)
70 Stuffed onions (Switzerland)
69 Stuffed peppers (Austria)
70 Stuffed sauerkraut (Rumania)
71 Viennese cauliflower (Austria)

Desserts and cakes

79 Almond crescents
91 Almond soup (Austria)
83 Appel pie (Hungary)
89 Apple pie from Thurgau (Switzerland)
80 Apple strudel (Austria)
78 Apricot dumplings (Austria)
91 Apricot soup (Austria)
84 Cake from Linz (Austria)
86 Cake from Sacher (Austria)
90 Carnivals fritters (Hungary)
91 Chestnut purée (Hungary)
90 Cottage cheese pie (Hungary)
78 Cream cheese crescents (Austria)
78 Crescents rolls (Austria)
86 Dobos cake (Austria)
82 Emperor's pancake (Austria)
83 Farmers pie from Uri (Switzerland)
87 Filbert pie from Solothurn (Switzerland)
78 Honey cookies (Switzerland)
90 Hungarian pancakes (Hungary)
87 Lazy cake (Hungary)
81 Marmor cake (Austria)
89 Monastery pie from St. Galler (Switzerland)

83 Moor in his shirt (Austria)
91 Müesli (Switzerland)
79 Nut crescents (Austria)
89 Pie with pears from Geneva (Switzerland)
77 Plum dumplings (Austria)
82 Poppy seed strudel (Hungary)
77 Snow balls (Austria)
82 Streusel cake (Hungary)
83 Tyrolean bread and butter pudding (Austria)
82 Vicarage pie (Switzerland)
89 Wine cake (Switzerland)

Beverages

93 Cardinal (Austria)
93 Chocolate with whipped cream (Austria)
93 Egg beer (Austria)
92 Spiced coffee Vienna style (Austria)
93 Wine punch (Austria)

Foreign languages:

Entrees

14 Böhmer Eierspeise (Austria)
14 Gefüllte kalte Eier (Austria)
14 Gerollte Eierspeise (Austria)
15 Kartoffelsalat (Austria)
15 Körözött (Czechoslovakia)
15 Rindfleischsalat (Austria)
13 Solothurner Käseschnitte (Switzerland)
12 Tiroler Eierspeise (Austria)

Cheese dishes

17 Fondue
17 Gâteau au fromage Fribourgeoise (Switzerland)
18 Jura Omelette (Switzerland)
17 Käse Beignet (Switzerland)
18 Käsekrapfen (Austria)

Soups

22 Aargauer Spinatsuppe (Switzerland)
21 Bárány leves (Hungary)
24 Bramborova polevka (Czechoslovakia)
21 Brotsuppe mit Eiern (Austria)
22 Erbsensuppe mit Schweinefleisch (Austria)
19 Gulyás leves (Hungary)
23 Gurkensuppe (Austria)
21 Hálaszlé (Hungary)
23 Houbova polevka (Czechoslovakia)
20 Hühnersuppe mit Leberknödel (Austria)
22 Kabis suppe (Switzerland)
24 Kaposztaleves (Hungary)
23 Kminova polevka (Czechoslovakia)
25 Kraftbrühe mit Griesznockerl (Austria)
20 Lebersuppe mit Rahm (Austria)
19 Paprikás leves (Hungary)
23 Paradiessuppe (Austria)
24 Urner Käsesuppe (Switzerland)
21 Wiener Fleischsuppe (Austria)
21 Wiener Kraftsuppe (Austria)

Dumplings

27 Aargauer Kartoffelpfluten (Switzerland)
26 Kartoffelknödel (Austria)
27 Leberknödel (Austria)
27 Nudelschöberl (Austria)
26 Nudelteig (Austria)
27 Schinkenfleckern (Austria)
26 Semmelknödel (Austria)

Fish dishes

35 Fischfilets nach Wiener Art (Austria)
39 Fisch mit Spargeln (Austria)
36 Fischragout (Austria)
34 Forellen mit Paradiesäpfeln (Austria)
32 Gebackener Karpfen (Austria)
35 Gefüllter Hecht (Austria)
38 Hal gombaval (Hungary)
38 Hal keszthely (Hungary)
35 Hecht in Kapernsauce (Austria)
38 Heringe Böhmer Art (Czechoslovakia)
34 Kalte Forellenfilets (Austria)
31 Kapr na cerno (Czechoslovakia)
30 Karpf im Rotwein (Austria)
31 Karpfen mit saurer Sahne (Austria)
31 Lachs nach Basler Art (Switzerland)
29 Paprika Karpfen (Austria)
39 Peste al bastru (Rumania)
28 Ponty leves (Hungary)
30 Bontypörkölt (Austria)
33 Salmone alla ticinese (Switzerland)
39 Schollenschnitzel (Austria)
34 Tiroler Forellen (Austria)

Meat dishes

47 Appenzellerli (Switzerland)
55 Berner Platte (Switzerland)
51 Bosnische schwarze Pfanne (Yugoslavia)
59 Chifteluta (Rumania)
60 Churer Fleischtorte (Switzerland)
54 Eingemachtes Kalbsfleisch (Austria)
48 Emmenthaler Schnitzel (Switzerland)
50 Eßterházy rostélyos (Hungary)
46 Gefüllter Kalbsbraten (Austria)
51 Gekochter Schweinschlegel (Austria)
49 Gespickte Kalbsvögerl (Austria)
41 Gulyas (Hungary)
56 Hammelkeule (Austria)
53 Kalbszunge (Austria)
43 Koloszvári gulyas (Hungary)
43 Krautfleisch (Austria)

43 Kümmelfleisch (Austria)
43 Majoran tokany (Hungary)
59 Mititei (Rumania)
59 Neuenburger Leberpastetchen (Switzerland)
54 Pieds de porc (Switzerland)
47 Pörkölt (Hungary)
46 Pörkölt Borjumaj (Hungary)
57 Potée Fribourgeoise (Switzerland)
42 Reisfleisch (Austria)
55 Rostélyos cigány módra (Hungary)
58 Schnitz und drunder (Switzerland)
52 Schweinekotelett auf Sauerkraut (Austria)
47 Steirisches Wurzelfleisch (Austria)
42 Székely gulyas (Hungary)
49 Tafelspitz (Austria)
54 Teleci gulas (Czechoslovakia)
46 Thurgauer Leberspätzli (Switzerland)
50 Tocana (Rumania)
59 Töltött káposzta (Hungary)
48 Wiener Schnitzel (Austria)
41 Znaimer Goulasch (Austria)
50 Znojemska pecene (Czechoslovakia)
44 Zürcher Geschnetzeltes (Switzerland)
58 Zürcher Ratsherrntopf (Switzerland)

Poultry and game dishes

66 Backhendl (Austria)
67 Coniglio arrosto alla ticinese (Switzerland)
63 Csirke Bácska (Hungary)
63 Csirke tejfolben (Hungary)
62 Eingemachtes Huhn (Austria)
67 Gebratene Gans (Austria)
66 Gebratenes Entchen (Austria)
63 Hühnerragout (Austria)
66 Kachnas cervenym-zelim (Czechoslovakia)
66 Kacsa kukoricaval (Rumania)
67 Kaninchenpastete (Austria)
63 Paprikás csirke (Hungary)
65 Pollo alla montanara (Switzerland)
61 Pui Românese (Rumania)
62 Sacher Huhn (Austria)

Vegetable dishes

74 Aargauer Rüeblitorte (Switzerland)
74 Burgunya paprikás (Hungary)
69 Gefüllte Paprikaschoten (Austria)
70 Gefüllte Zwiebeln (Switzerland)
71 Karfiol Wiener Art (Austria)
73 Krautstrudel (Austria)
75 Mamaliga (Rumania)
71 Papet Vaudois (Switzerland)
72 Paprika Tomaten Gemüse (Austria)
69 Reis mit Bohnen (Austria)
75 Repasaláta (Hungary)
74 Rösti (Switzerland)
75 Salate de vinete (Rumania)
70 Sarmalutsa (Rumania)
74 Schaffhauser Bölletünne (Switzerland)
71 Spinat Pizokel (Switzerland)
75 Spárgasaláta (Hungary)

Desserts and cakes

83 Almas Pite (Hungary)
80 Apfelstrudel (Austria)
79 Buchteln (Austria)
86 Dobostorta (Hungary)
90 Faschingskrapfen (Austria)
91 Gesztenyepure (Hungary)
81 Gugelhupf (Austria)
78 Honigleckerli (Switzerland)
82 Kaiserschmarren (Austria)
78 Kipfeln (Austria)
84 Linzer Torte (Austria)
87 Lusta torta (Hungary)
82 Makosrétes (Hungary)
91 Mandelsuppe (Austria)
78 Marillenknödel (Austria)
91 Marillensuppe (Austria)
91 Müesli (Switzerland)
83 Mohr im Hemd (Austria)
79 Nusskipfeln (Austria)
90 Palacsinta (Hungary)
77 Pflaumenknödel (Austria)
86 Sachertorte (Austria)
77 Schneenockerl (Austria)
87 Solothurner Nusskuchen (Switzerland)
89 St. Galler Klostertorte (Switzerland)
82 Streuselkuchen (Austria)
89 Tarte aux poires à la Genevoise (Switzerland)
89 Thurgauer Apfeltorte (Switzerland)
83 Tiroler Scheiterhaufen (Austria)
78 Topfenkipfeln (Austria)
90 Túróslepény (Hungary)
83 Urner Bauernpastete (Switzerland)
89 Weintorte (Switzerland)
82 Zürcher Pfarrhaustorte (Switzerland)

Beverages

93 Eierbier (Austria)
93 Glühwein (Austria)
93 Kakao mit Schlagobers (Austria)
93 Kardinal (Austria)
92 Wiener Kaffee (Austria)

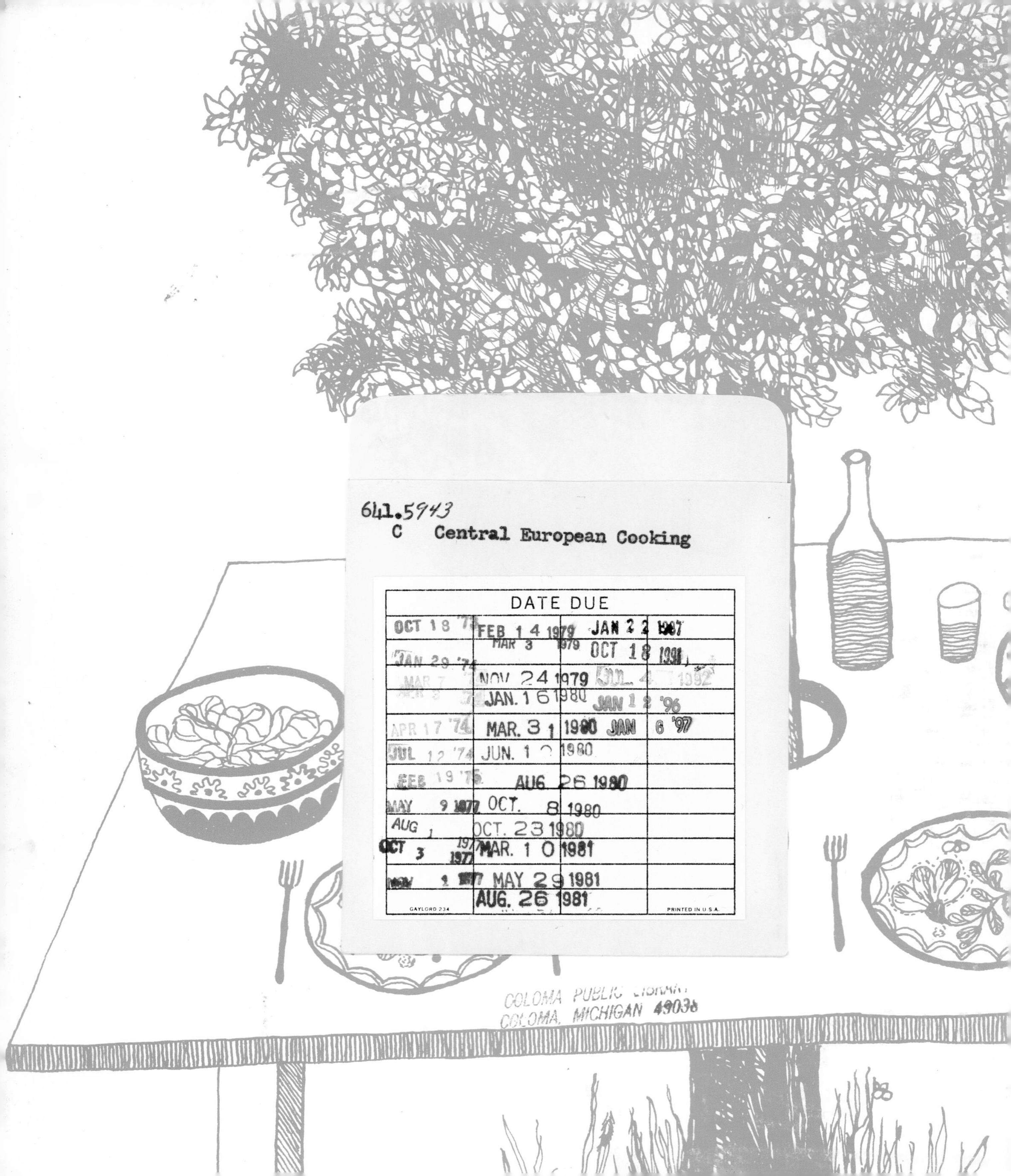